D0849386

DATE DUE

MAY 1 9 2014			

LIVING THROUGH

THE MEXICAN-AMERICAN WAR

John DiConsiglio

www.capstonepub.com
Visit our website to find out more information about Heinemann-Raintree books.

To order:
☎ Phone 888-454-2279
🖥 Visit www.capstonepub.com
to browse our catalog and order online.

Edited by Adam Miller and Megan Cotugno
Designed by Steve Mead
Original illustrations © Capstone Global Library Ltd
Picture research by Ruth Blair
Production by Eirian Griffiths
Originated by Capstone Global Library Ltd
Printed and bound in the United States of America, North Mankato, MN
15 14 13 12
10 9 8 7 6 5 4 3

Library of Congress Cataloging-in-Publication Data
DiConsiglio, John.
  The Mexican-American War / John DiConsiglio.
    p. cm.—(Living through...)
  Includes bibliographical references and index.
  ISBN 978-1-4329-5998-2 (hb)—ISBN 978-1-4329-6007-0 (pb) 1. Mexican War, 1846-1848—Juvenile literature. I. Title.
  E404.D53 2012
  973.6'2—dc23   2011016817

112012
006963RP

Acknowledgments
The author and publishers are grateful to the following for permission to reproduce copyright material: ©Art Archive: pp. 18 (Culver Pictures), 32 (National History Museum Mexico City / Gianni Dagli Orti), 50 (Culver Pictures), 62 (Gianni Dagli Orti); ©akg-images: pp. 12 (North Wind Picture Archives), 43 (North Wind Picture Archives), 45 (North Wind Picture Archives), 59 (Interfoto / Sammlung Rauch), 61 (ullstein bild); ©Corbis: pp. 16, 21 (© Bettmann), 27, 33, 41 (© Bettmann), 47 (© Carl & Ann Purcell); ©Getty Images: pp. 5 (Kean Collection), 9 (Hulton Archive), 23 (Alexander Hesler/George Eastman House), 30 (MPI), 35 (Buyenlarge), 46 (Hulton Archive), 48 (MPI); ©Library of Congress: pp. 25 (N. Currier), 28 (N. Currier), 37 (Currier & Ives), 38, 57.

Cover photograph reproduced with permission from Corbis (© Bettmann).

We would like to thank Strother Roberts for his invaluable help in the preparation of this book.

Every effort has been made to contact copyright holders of any material reproduced in this book. Any omissions will be rectified in subsequent printings if notice is given to the publisher.

All the Internet addresses (URLs) given in this book were valid at the time of going to press. However, due to the dynamic nature of the Internet, some addresses may have changed, or sites may have changed or ceased to exist since publication. While the author and publisher regret any inconvenience this may cause readers, no responsibility for any such changes can be accepted by either the author or the publisher.

CONTENTS

Words printed in **bold** are explained in the Glossary.

A WAR OF CONTRADICTIONS

It was among the most popular wars in U.S. history.[1] It was hailed by the U.S. president at the time, James K. Polk, as nothing less than a mission from God.[2] Tens of thousands of young men hurried to **enlist** and become instant heroes.[3] When it was over, U.S. land would stretch across North America, "from sea to shining sea."

It was the Mexican-American War (1846–48). Today, it is an almost forgotten conflict, squeezed between the American Revolution and the Civil War. But the U.S. war with Mexico is among the most pivotal moments for both nations. It saw a young United States flex its military muscles for the first time, even as the Mexican **Republic** began to fade into the shadows of history.

The war's cast of characters included future Civil War heroes such as Ulysses S. Grant and Robert E. Lee, while young politicians such as Illinois Congressman Abraham Lincoln would rise to fame. In the end, Mexico would lose half its land. The United States would expand by more than 1 million square miles (2.6 million square kilometers). New states—including Texas and California—would join the growing union.

OPPOSITION TO WAR

But not everyone saw the war as a rousing victory for the young United States. In fact, it is still controversial today. An outspoken U.S. peace movement bitterly opposed the war. Some saw it as a tragic theft of Mexican land. Others believed the war was a plot to extend slavery into new states—something much of the North was opposed to at the time. Lincoln delivered antiwar speeches on the floors of Congress. Poet Henry David Thoreau went to jail as a protest against the war.

In Mexico, people today still consider the war to be an act of aggression. In fact, it is known there as *La Invasión Estadounidense de México* ("The American Invasion of Mexico").[4] The humbling loss to the United States still affects the way many Mexicans think about their history.[5]

Few wars have **incited** as much passion as the Mexican-American War. The United States won a clear victory. But the conflict left the nation divided. Its wounds were so deep that a Civil War would then tear the country apart.[6]

△ Remember the Alamo? Santa Anna's 3,000 troops slaughtered 200 Texans at the fort. The massacre united the Texas settlers against Mexico.

TENSIONS RISE

In the early 1800s, Mexico and the United States were large neighboring countries. But these neighbors had very different borders and territories than they do today (see map).

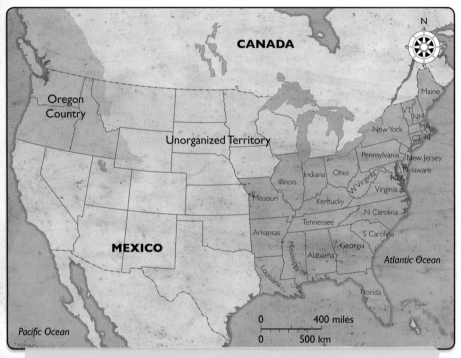

△ This map shows North America circa 1830. At the time, the U.S. consisted of 27 states. Mexico owned Texas and most of the west, including all or part of California, Nevada, Utah, New Mexico, Arizona, Colorado, and Wyoming.

Mexico was a proud nation. Its capital, Mexico City, had been the heart of the **Aztec Empire** for about a century. Long before the pilgrims landed in Massachusetts, Mexico had been a home to universities, hospitals, and theaters.[1]

In the 1500s, Spanish explorer Hernán Cortés slaughtered the Aztecs and claimed Mexico for Spain. The nation remained under Spanish control for 300 years. But in 1821 Mexico won a 10-year war for independence.

In the mid-1850s, Mexico spanned about 2 million square miles (3.2 million square kilometers) across the continent. Its population was just 8 million, but its land stretched through Texas into what is today the western United States: California, Nevada, Utah, and large portions of New Mexico, Arizona, Colorado, and Wyoming.

In its own northern lands, Mexicans were largely outnumbered. Americans flooded into Texas. American Indian tribes lived west of the Mississippi River—along with hundreds of white U.S. settlers who drove covered wagons through what maps labeled the "Great American Desert."[2]

Mexico's government was unstable at this time. After years of Spanish rule, no Mexican leader was able to hold on to control for long. In 1846 alone, the presidency changed hands three times.[3]

THE EARLY UNITED STATES

During this same period, the United States was rising. The country had been formed just about 70 years earlier, after the Revolutionary War with Great Britain. The new United States was a "go-ahead nation," according to historians.[4] While still mostly a farming country, the United States was becoming modernized, thanks to the **Industrial Revolution**. Innovations were becoming popular, from the locomotive to the sewing machine.[5]

In the mid-1800s, the U.S. population was about 20 million. That is about the same as New York state today. There were just 27 stars on the U.S. flag, one for each state. And its western border ran roughly from present-day Wisconsin to Louisiana. Beyond that to the west— all the way to the Pacific Ocean—was another country: Mexico.[6]

After earning its independence from Great Britain, the young United States did not crown a king. Instead, it elected representatives to make laws, and a president to enforce the laws. It created a republic—a government run by the people. Americans had boundless ambition. In their minds, they could do anything. Nothing could stand in their way.

In this way, these two neighbors—Mexico and the United States— seemed to live in two different worlds. And these two worlds were about to collide.

THE LONE STAR PROBLEM

After gaining independence from Spain in 1821, Mexico had enormous tracts of territory to govern. The most troublesome area was a dry wasteland called Texas. Settlers were discouraged by its searing heat, its unwelcome landscape, and, most of all, the near-constant raids by American Indian tribes. By 1825 only about 3,500 Mexicans lived in Texas.[7]

The Mexican government wanted to fill the empty land and discourage Comanche Indian attacks. So, Mexico invited U.S. settlers to move to Texas. They offered the travelers generous land grants. In return, Mexico asked the "Texians," as they were called, to follow some conditions. The settlers had to become Mexican citizens and follow Mexican law. Parts of the United States still allowed slavery, but "Texians" were expected to leave their slaves on the U.S. side of the border.[8]

The first land grant went to a banker from Missouri named Moses Austin. He died before he could gather other settlers, and his son, Stephen F. Austin, inherited the grant. The 29-year-old was determined to take over the Mexican territory with "North American population, enterprise [hard work], and intelligence." Austin led 300 families into Texas, opening the pioneer floodgates.[9]

Quickly, the new settlers overwhelmed the native Spanish-speaking population by nearly 10 to 1. Austin lured 20,000 Americans to Texas.[10] By 1834 Texas's population had grown to nearly 38,000 people. But only 8,000 were Mexican citizens.[11]

SANTA ANNA

Texans were taking advantage of the region's wide-open spaces, using the land for animal grazing and farming. But the unruly U.S. settlers had little interest in following Mexican laws. They refused to learn Spanish, and they maintained their own separate schools. Worst of all, settlers openly ignored the law against having slaves.[12]

Soon, Mexico had seen enough. It barred new U.S. **immigrants**. It imposed harsh laws on the Texans, including high property taxes, **tariffs** on U.S.-shipped goods, and a strong crackdown on slavery. Still, Americans continued to flow into the Texas territory.

In 1833 General Antonio López de Santa Anna became the president of Mexico. He announced that he would no longer tolerate the rebellious U.S. settlers. Austin responded by encouraging Texans to arm themselves and prepare for a fight. Texas declared its independence from Mexico in 1836.

Santa Anna and his Mexican army were not about to give the Texans their independence. But Austin had many U.S. volunteers on his side, along with Mexicans who opposed Santa Anna.

THE ALAMO

In 1835 a squad of Texas soldiers had captured a Mexican-held fort in Texas called the Alamo. On February 23, 1836, Santa Anna led 1,500 Mexican soldiers to the Alamo, determined to take it back. Only about 200 Texans defended the Alamo, including David Crockett and Jim Bowie.

△ Stephen F. Austin, the "Father of Texas," opened the floodgates to settlements when he led 300 pioneer families into the region.

The Mexican army surrounded the fort and fired cannonballs over its walls. The hopelessly outnumbered Texans held strong through a 13-day siege, vowing never to surrender. But on March 6, Santa Anna's soldiers finally stormed the Alamo. All but two Texan fighters were slaughtered. The assault sparked outrage, inspiring people in Texas—and throughout the United States—to vow revenge.

THE BATTLE OF SAN JACINTO

Santa Anna pushed his troops deeper into Texas. But the newly organized Texan army, boosted by hundreds of U.S. volunteers, met the general in April at the Battle of San Jacinto. Texan General Sam Houston easily defeated Santa Anna's forces in a fight that lasted just 18 minutes. The Texan soldiers shouted, "Remember the Alamo!" as they sent off the Mexican army. About 700 of the Mexican soldiers were killed, while just 9 Texans died.

THE REPUBLIC OF TEXAS

Santa Anna was captured the following day and held prisoner. Three weeks later, while in jail, he signed a peace **treaty**. It recognized Texas's independence and ordered the Mexican army to leave the area. The treaty also made a river called the Rio Grande become the boundary between Texas and Mexico. The border between Texas and the United States had always been the Nueces River, which was about 160 miles (257 kilometers) further north of the Rio Grande.

For nearly 10 years the Republic of Texas was an independent country. It was recognized by the United States, France, the Netherlands, and Belgium. But Mexico refused to accept the loss of Texas. It still claimed the region as a Mexican territory. In its eyes, the Texans were rebels.

Mexico sternly warned the United States to not even consider **annexing** Texas, making it a state. Mexico was clear. That action would lead to war.

"STILL, THEY DREAM ON"

A woman named Frances Calderon de la Barca wrote of life in Mexico during the period leading up to the Mexican-American War. She was the Scottish wife of the Spanish **ambassador** to Mexico, and they arrived in Mexico in 1840. She admired the nation's centuries-old stone castles and the soaring steeples of Catholic churches.[13]

But in letters to her family—later collected in a book called *Life in Mexico*—Calderon also noted that 1840s Mexico was a country divided. Mexico's leaders were often military generals. Much of the nation's money was in the hands of wealthy **aristocrats**, who ruled over huge farms called plantations.[14]

But most Mexicans were not rich landowners. They were poor. Many were farmers, merchants, and Indians living off the land. The government changed hands several times during the unstable years following its independence in 1821, but living conditions never improved for most Mexicans.

Calderon walked through the "ill-paved courtyards" of Mexico City and saw "nothing but groups of peasants or of beggars."[15] She wrote: "Here everything reminds us of the past. It is the present that seems like a dream."[16]

When General Santa Anna seized control of the Mexican government in 1840, Calderon wrote that Mexico City's merchants and peasants barely seemed to notice, let alone care. She wrote. "In what other city in the world would they not have taken part with one side or the other?"[17]

"All is decaying and growing fainter," Calderon wrote of the aging Mexico. "Men seem trusting to some unknown future that they will never see. . . . Still, they dream on."[18]

THE PIONEER LIFE

Morris Schaff was born on an Ohio farm in 1840.[19] It was an exciting time in U.S. history. The young nation was changing rapidly. The new steam locomotive allowed Americans to travel great distances in just weeks. The first **telegraph** lines were strung between Baltimore, Maryland, and Washington, D.C.

By the time Schaff was six years old, the United States was at war with Mexico. Much of the country was reading Edgar Allan Poe's mysterious poem "The Raven." A young U.S. writer named Herman Melville published a high-seas adventure novel called *Typee*. Five years later, he would write his most famous work, *Moby-Dick*. In 1846 the first game of baseball was played. During this period, P. T. Barnum's American Museum—advertised as "all that is monstrous, scaley, strange and queer"—took New York City by storm.[20]

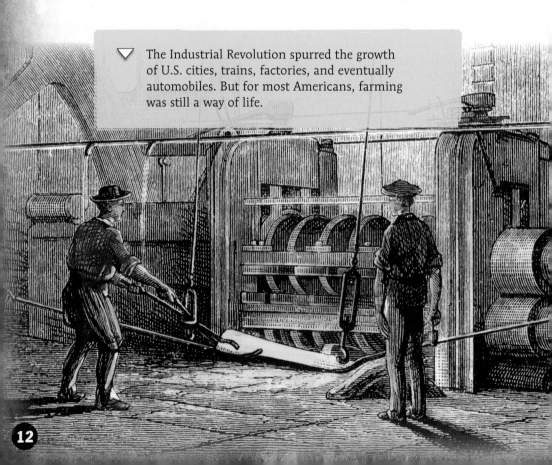

▽ The Industrial Revolution spurred the growth of U.S. cities, trains, factories, and eventually automobiles. But for most Americans, farming was still a way of life.

THE INDUSTRIAL REVOLUTION

The Industrial Revolution was turning the United States into a country of bustling cities, trains, and factories. But for most young Americans, farming was still a way of life.

In Etna Township, Ohio, Schaff got up before dawn and helped his father work on the farm. He was amazed by the tall trees surrounding the landscape, even as he helped his father clear tracts of forest to harvest more land. Schaff spent his afternoons catching crickets in the woods and watching flocks of pigeons fly overhead. He was in awe of the new national road being built through the state. It promised to open the township to stagecoaches and herds of livestock heading west.[21]

But the Ohio countryside was not completely peaceful. One day, young Schaff saw flashing lights in the horizon. When he climbed over nearby hills, he found a uniformed **militia** company—volunteer soldiers. Schaff didn't know it, but they were about to be shipped off to fight in the Mexican-American War. More than 50 years later, Schaff wrote about the wide-eyed child who was captivated by the training soldiers:

*In my eyes, as this company paraded west of the schoolhouse in Etna Village, they looked like warriors of many a bloody field; and when they came marching along with their flintlock **muskets** with savage-looking fixed **bayonets**—keeping step to two screaming fifes ... and a bass drum beaten in lofty style ... Where is the rustic heart that would not beat fast at such a spectacle of martial [military] glory? Thumping with great flourishes and casting from time to time a fierce look at us small boys chasing along in bulging-eyed awe.[22]*

MILITARY CAREER

The soldiers made a lasting impression on Schaff. His mind was made up: He would someday join the U.S. Army. He attended the military academy at West Point, and he then fought in the Civil War under generals like Ulysses S. Grant.

After his military career, Schaff wrote history books. But he also described his Ohio boyhood. He wrote about watching wild turkeys run through fields and woods that would soon be plowed or cut down.[23] War was on the horizon, and Schaff was growing up. The United States would never be the same again.

COUNTDOWN TO WAR

In 1844 one question was on every American's lips. As the presidential election approached, voters asked: "Who is James K. Polk?"

In some ways the answer was easy. Polk, a congressman from Tennessee, was part of the Democratic Party. He had served four years as speaker of the House of Representatives. But he was still a virtual unknown when he ran for president.

The rival **Whig Party**, sensing an easy victory, taunted him with shouts of: "Who is James K. Polk?"[1] Yet Polk managed to become the 11th president of the United States. The outcome of the election shocked politicians. But Polk was a clever campaigner. He had tapped into a rising tide that was sweeping the nation: expansion fever.

Manifest Destiny

In 1845 a New York publisher named John O'Sullivan first coined the phrase "Manifest Destiny," when he wrote that it was the United States' "manifest destiny to overspread and to possess the whole of the continent."[2]

O'Sullivan meant that the United States was on a mission to spread democracy—"the great experiment of liberty,"[3] as he called it—throughout North America. But the idea was soon used to justify the country's westward expansion into Texas and California. Passionate political speeches, mostly by Democrats, created an almost religious feeling about Manifest Destiny.

Critics had other ideas. They saw Manifest Destiny as nothing more than an attempt to take land from other nations. They also saw it as a way to create new territories that allowed slavery, an issue that was increasingly dividing the North from the South in the United States (see page 20).

MANIFEST DESTINY

Americans had taken hold of an idea called "**Manifest Destiny**." The way many Americans saw it, their democratic system was the best form of government in the world. They felt it was their God-given right—even their duty—to expand the country's borders.[4]

Polk appealed to the "Manifest Destiny" wave. While other presidential candidates opposed annexing Texas, Polk promised that, if elected, he would bring Texas into the union—along with California and the rest of the West.

The U.S. political landscape

In the 1840s, two political parties dominated the U.S. political landscape: the Whigs and the Democrats. A third party, the Republican Party, was only just beginning.

Democrats
Famous founders: Thomas Jefferson, Andrew Jackson
What they supported: States' rights, limited government, an agricultural economy, slavery, expansion into new territory
Whom they represented: Southerners, farmers, immigrants, westerners in favor of gaining more land, some pro-states'-rights northerners

Whigs
Famous founders: John Quincy Adams, Henry Clay
What they supported: **Industrialization**, more power for Congress than for the president, outlawing slavery (this was true of most Whigs)
Whom they represented: The northern middle class (mostly New England and New York), skilled workers, people opposed to slavery

Republicans
Famous founder: Abraham Lincoln
What they supported: Outlawing slavery, a powerful central government, industrialization, high tariffs on imported goods
Whom they represented: Ex-Whigs, abolitionists, northerners, industry

POLK AND TEXAS

Polk would make good on his campaign promise. By the end of his term, the United States would stretch from the Atlantic Ocean to the Pacific Ocean. The first step was to take Texas. On July 4, 1845, Texans voted overwhelmingly to join the United States.

Countries like Great Britain and France may have recognized Texas as an independent nation, but not Mexico. It considered Texas to be a rebellious territory and still part of Mexico—not the United States.

President Polk expected the Mexican army to overrun Texas. He was taking no chances. By October 1845, Polk stationed 3,000 troops along the Rio Grande. Mexico accused the U.S. soldiers of invading their country. The United States insisted it was just protecting Texan soil.

A COUNTEROFFER

With both sides poised for war, Polk made one last stab at a nonviolent resolution. Instead of fighting over the land, he tried to buy it. On November 10, Polk sent Louisiana trader John Slidell on a secret mission to Mexico City. Slidell was instructed to offer $30 million for what is today Texas, California, and much of New Mexico.

President Polk sent Louisiana trader John Slidell on a secret mission to obtain Mexican land. When the government failed to meet him, Slidell insisted Mexico be "chastised."

The Louisiana Purchase

In the years leading up to war, Mexico had an enormous amount of land, but not enough people to fill it. The struggle for independence from Spain throughout the early 1800s had devastated the Mexican economy and cut through its population.

In contrast, the United States was growing—both economically and in terms of its population. It needed more land to grow, and it had the money to pay for it.

To create room for its expanding needs in the past, the United States had purchased most of its territory. In 1803 President Thomas Jefferson bought more than 800,000 square miles (2.1 million square kilometers) from France, in a deal known as the Louisiana Purchase. The new land covered 14 present-day states. The United States had expectations that this sort of transaction could work again with Mexico—but this was not the case.

One of Mexico's greatest resources was land (see box)—almost 1.5 million square miles (3.9 million square kilometers). But Mexico would not sell it. It was a matter of national honor and pride for Mexico to keep its territory in one piece. Mexico had defeated the great Spanish Empire. Many Mexicans were insulted that the upstart United States was trying to take their land, whether it paid for it or not.[5]

Slidell waited for weeks in Mexico City to meet with the president. But as he anxiously counted the days, the Mexican government was overthrown by a military coup. The new president, General Mariano Paredes y Arrillaga, had no interest in negotiating with the Americans.

Slidell had waited long enough. He returned to the United States and delivered a stinging report to Polk. There was no reasoning with Mexico, he insisted. He urged the president to make a military response to Mexico's insulting rejection. The Mexicans, Slidell said, had to be "chastised [punished]."[6] What the United States couldn't buy, it would take by force.

On December 29, Polk defied Mexico's warning about annexing Texas, when he made it the 28th state. He set the United States on a path that would lead to war.

GENERAL TAYLOR

Tensions mounted along the Rio Grande. Mexican soldiers and U.S. troops were stationed on opposite banks of the river. Their guns were aimed at the enemy. Each waited for the other to make the first move.

General Zachary Taylor (see box) led the Texan troops. A rugged veteran, the 62-year-old Taylor had served as a U.S. Army officer in the War of 1812, a war fought against the British Empire over territory, among other issues. He gained a reputation as a fierce fighter in campaigns against the Seminoles, a group of American Indians, in the 1830s.

BIOGRAPHY

Zachary Taylor
1784–1850

BORN: Barboursville, Virginia

ROLE: U.S. general and president

General Zachary Taylor was nicknamed "Old Rough and Ready." Wearing a straw hat with his uniform, his troops said Taylor looked more like an old farmer than a general.[7] In a time when military leaders rarely fought alongside ordinary soldiers, Taylor was beloved by his men. Riding atop an ivory stallion named "Old Whitey," Taylor famously rode alongside his soldiers, urging them into battle.

Taylor was the top U.S. general in early battles against Mexico. His victories, often against seemingly impossible odds, made him a renowned war hero. In 1848 he was elected president.

Taylor in battle

"Old Rough and Ready," as Taylor was nicknamed, was famous for his battlefield bravery. As Samuel McNeil, an Ohio shoemaker in Taylor's army, wrote in 1847:

I must mention one circumstance that happened ... which shows the extraordinary coolness of Gen. Z. Taylor in battle. He saw a small cannon ball coming directly towards his person. Instead of spurring [his horse] "Old Whitey" out of its way, he coolly rose in his very short stirrups and permitted the ball to pass between his person and the saddle.[8]

THE THORNTON AFFAIR

As days passed, Mexico's forces grew. By mid-April, 1846, about 6,000 *soldados* ("soldiers") were entrenched along the Rio Grande, more than twice the number of Taylor's troops. General Mariano Arista sent a letter to Taylor, warning that it was only a matter of time before his forces crossed the Rio Grande and wiped out Taylor's "Army of **Occupation**."

Taylor held his ground. True to his word, Arista ordered a 2,000-strong Mexican **cavalry** to cross the Rio Grande. They surprised a 70-man U.S. patrol led by Captain Seth Thornton. The patrol was no match for the Mexican soldiers. Thornton and 16 of his men were slaughtered.

Taylor relayed the news back to Polk. Mexican soldiers had massacred Americans. The "Thornton Affair" was the last straw. The threat of conflict had loomed over both countries. Now it was inevitable. The United States and Mexico were at war.

"AMERICAN BLOOD UPON AMERICAN SOIL"

After the Thornton Affair, Polk was ready to lead the United States into war. On May 11, 1846, the president addressed Congress. He explained: "Mexico has passed the boundary of the United States, has invaded our territory and shed American blood upon American soil."[9] He called for a declaration of war. On May 13, after debating just a few hours, Congress agreed and voted to declare war on Mexico.

The United States of the 1840s was divided between the North and South (see box). Southern Democrats lined up in full force behind the war effort. Polk's Democrats were energized by their belief in Manifest Destiny. The South also wanted new territory as a buffer against the fast-growing North. That new land would come from Mexico—whether it was in Texas or in the Mexican-owned western lands like California and New Mexico.

Many Americans also craved new land for a more practical reason: money. Americans in the early 1800s depended on land for their livelihoods. Poor farmers grew crops and raised livestock to feed their families. Middle-class farmers produced enough to sell any surplus (extra) goods—often sugar or cotton—at local markets. More westward territory meant more land—and more profits.[10]

North vs. South

At the onset of the war, Americans were increasingly divided over slavery. The division separated North and South. Southerners, largely aligned with Polk's Democratic Party, relied on slavery for their agricultural economy. Southern people used slaves to tend to their acres of fields. The industrialized North was growing fast. It was strongly tied to the antislavery Whigs, who favored industrialization rather than acquiring more farmland. These divisions over slavery extended to divisions over the war with Mexico.

WAR FEVER

Instantly, many Americans were gripped with war fever. At the outbreak of the war, the U.S. Army consisted of fewer than 9,000 officers and men. Congress authorized the president to call up 50,000 volunteers.[11] They were handed guns and uniforms. Then, after only a few days of training, they were shipped to Mexico.

Hundreds of thousands of additional young men rushed to enlist. They came from all walks of life—from the sons of famous politicians and descendents of wealthy families with Revolutionary War ties to poor farmers, Irish immigrants, and even a few American Indians.[12] At New York recruiting offices, signs bore the slogan "Mexico or Death."[13] The response was so overwhelming that thousands of volunteers were turned away.

As they prepared to leave for Mexico, the troops were celebrated with firework displays and flag-waving crowds. Their actions were hailed in songs. Young U.S. writers like *Last of the Mohicans* author James Fenimore Cooper wrote books about their bravery on the battlefield.[14] Americans were cheering their soldiers to war. They expected a fast victory.

▷ James Fenimore Cooper (1789–1851) wrote books about the bravery of the American troops during the Mexican-American War.

THE PEACE MOVEMENT

Tens of thousands of Americans hurried off to fight in Mexico, gripped by patriotism. But not everyone joined the war effort. Some loud and determined voices strongly opposed the war. They saw it as a plot to take land from a **sovereign** nation. They worried that the United States was the actual aggressor, unjustly invading Mexico.

To Whigs—and even some of Polk's own Democrats—the president was acting too quickly. They felt that Polk was bullying another nation into fighting for its own land. "Let us put a check upon this lust of dominion [power]," said Congressman Robert Toombs, of Georgia. "We had territory enough, Heaven knew."[15]

Joshua Giddings, a Pennsylvania congressman, called the war with Mexico "an aggressive, unholy, and unjust war."[16] He even voted against supplying soldiers with weapons. "In the murder of Mexicans upon their own soil, or in robbing them of their country, I can take no part," he said. Whig leader Henry Clay declared, "This is no war of defense, but one of unnecessary and offensive aggression."[17]

Civil disobedience

Many writers and poets opposed the war, from Walt Whitman to Ralph Waldo Emerson. A young essayist and poet named Henry David Thoreau was sent to jail when he refused to pay his taxes as an antiwar protest.

One of the great writers in U.S. history, Thoreau later wrote an essay entitled "Civil Disobedience." In it, he declared that everyone had a duty to protest immoral laws. His work inspired many people who supported peace, including Mahatma Gandhi and Martin Luther King, Jr. Thoreau spent just one night in jail before his aunt paid his taxes—against Thoreau's wishes. While in jail, Thoreau was visited by Emerson. When Emerson asked, "Henry, why are you here?" Thoreau replied, "Why are you not here?"[18]

"Spotty Lincoln"

Before Abraham Lincoln became the first Republican president, he was a Whig congressman from Illinois. Like many other Whigs, Lincoln attacked Polk for wrongly provoking a war with Mexico. He pointed out that Mexico might not have shed "American blood" on "American soil" after all. The Thornton Affair (see page 18) had taken place in disputed territory claimed by both countries. "That soil was not ours!" Lincoln proclaimed. He challenged Polk to prove that Thornton's patrol was attacked on U.S. land. "Show me the spot [of the assault]!," Lincoln demanded.[19]

War advocates questioned Lincoln's patriotism. They mocked his "spot" speech with nicknames like "Spotty Lincoln" and "the Ranchero Spotty."[20]

△ Before becoming president, Lincoln was so strongly opposed to the Mexican War that some voters questioned his patriotism.

But Lincoln stuck by his claims. In Congress, he voted against the war—although he supported sending supplies to the troops.

Still, Lincoln could not shake a reputation as being a traitor to his country during the war with Mexico.[21] He lost his congressional reelection bid—but rallied by winning the presidency in 1860 and 1864.

Others said the war was just an excuse to expand slavery into new territories. In the North, antislavery forces called abolitionists condemned the war as a scheme to extend slavery to more territories. Even former president John Quincy Adams accused southerners of using the war to expand slavery into new land—and to increase their power in the government.

THE WAR IN TEXAS AND MEXICO

Even before war was officially declared on May 13, 1846, the U.S. and Mexican armies began fighting in the thick trees and bushes—or *chaparral*—lining the Rio Grande.

The Americans dug in at a small area they called Fort Texas. On May 3, General Taylor heard reports that Mexicans planned to **ambush** a nearby supply depot. He gathered the bulk of his troops and raced to head off the attackers.

As soon as Taylor left, Mexican **artillery** pounded the fort, shelling it with a six-day cannonball attack. Miraculously, only two Americans were killed, including the fort's commander, Major Jacob Brown. Fort Texas was renamed Fort Brown in his honor.

Battlefield medicine

Doctors and surgeons traveled with troops during the war. But they did not understand infection and made no attempt to keep wounds sterile (clean)—even during surgery. They rarely washed their hands or instruments before moving to the next bed. No **antibiotics** were available. Minor wounds became deadly infections. Soldiers actually faced a greater risk of dying from disease and infections than from battle wounds.

Men with serious torso injuries were doomed to die. When an overworked surgeon encountered a limb shattered by a musket ball, he had just one option: **amputation**. Exhausted doctors performed hundreds of amputations, some in as little as 10 minutes. Surgeons worked around the clock—producing piles of amputated limbs.[1]

Lieutenant Daniel Harvey Hill, a soldier in General Taylor's 4th Artillery, recalled hearing the agonizing cries of wounded men in cramped, dirty hospital tents. "The suffering of the sick in the crowded hospital tents were horrible beyond conception," he wrote.[2]

At the battle of Palo Alto, General Taylor used his military cunning to lead his out-numbered troops to victory.

THE BATTLE OF PALO ALTO

On May 8, Taylor and 2,400 troops hurried back to aid the troops at Fort Brown. But General Arista and 3,400 *soldados* blocked the road. The troops met at Palo Alto, 8 miles (13 kilometers) north of the Rio Grande. The stage was set for the first major battle of the war.

Taylor's troops would have surged forward with bayonets. But Arista's army was stretched 1 mile (1.6 kilometers) wide. It would be almost impossible to charge into their ranks. Instead, Taylor used a new tactic. He called it "flying artillery." Armed horse-riding soldiers cut through the thick brush in a speedy attack-and-retreat motion. Their lightweight guns could fire every 10 to 15 seconds, more than five times faster than Mexican artillery. Suffering heavy casualties, Arista was forced back across the river.

The next day, 3 miles (5 kilometers) north of the Rio Grande, the two armies met again at Resaca de la Palma. The Mexicans were firmly entrenched along a shallow stream, hidden in the chaparral. The two sides waged a fierce hand-to-hand battle.

The Mexicans were forced to abandon their post—including their artillery. Some Mexican soldiers drowned as they desperately tried to swim across the Rio Grande. Taylor's men swarmed through the Mexican camp. General Arista's cooks had already prepared a victory meal. That night, U.S. soldiers ate it instead.[3]

SARAH BORGINNIS: "THE HEROINE OF FORT BROWN"

The history books are filled with the stories of hardworking women who supported the U.S. war effort against Mexico—whether at home or on the battlefield. Although exact numbers are unknown, experts say that hundreds of women followed troops as cooks, nurses, and laundresses. Most of them were the wives of soldiers. Some actually took care of their infant children while accompanying their husbands.[5]

Women in combat

A handful of women may actually have seen combat in the Mexican-American War. Eliza Ann Billings claimed to have disguised herself as a man and joined the invasion of Mexico City (see pages 60 and 61). Although she wrote a popular memoir, most historians question Billing's story.[4]

The most famous female fighter of the war was Sarah Borginnis. When her husband enlisted in General Taylor's army, Borginnis signed on as a laundress. Her job was to cook and clean the company's uniforms.[6]

Standing more than 6 feet (182 centimeters) tall and weighing 200 pounds (91 kilograms), Borginnis was nicknamed "the Great Western," probably because she was said to be as sturdy as a similarly named U.S. ship. The tough-talking Borginnis wasn't shy about her desire to join the fighting. If men let her, she proclaimed, she'd "whip every scoundrel" in the Mexican army.[7]

COURAGE UNDER FIRE

In 1846 Borginnis had followed her husband to Fort Texas (later called Fort Brown; see page 24). When the Mexican army attacked, most of the company's laundresses were sent to bunkers, where they sewed sandbags. Rather than taking shelter, Borginnis remained with the soldiers. Amid the gunfire, she cooked their meals and attended to the sick. When a stray bullet pierced her bonnet, Borginnis, undeterred, continued bringing the soldiers buckets of coffee—while wearing the bullet-riddled bonnet. When a newspaper reporter heard the tale, Borginnis was nicknamed the "Heroine of Fort Brown."[8]

Borginnis followed the Army into northern Mexico. She later saw action in the Battle of Buena Vista (see page 36). As the bullets flew, she raced among the soldiers, bringing food and coffee, reloading weapons, and carrying the wounded to safety. According to some accounts, Borginnis was slashed on the cheek with a Mexican saber— and, reportedly, she responded by firing a cannonball at her attacker.[9]

In 1866 Borginnis died from a poisonous spider bite—some say it was a tarantula. She was held in such esteem that she was named an honorary colonel and buried with full military honors.[10]

▽ Sarah Borginnis's courage under-fire during the Battle of Buena Vista (pictured below) earned her the nickname the "Heroine of Fort Brown."

THE BATTLE OF MONTERREY

After victories at Palo Alto and Resaca de la Palma, General Taylor had the Mexican army on the run. The new Mexican commander-in-chief, General Pedro de Ampudia, retreated south to an **impenetrable** fortress—the walled city of Monterrey, in northeastern Mexico.

The mighty Monterrey was heavily **fortified** by thick stone walls. As Taylor led 2,300 U.S. troops across the Rio Grande in pursuit of Ampudia, the Mexican general gathered his forces. During the summer of 1846, Taylor was forced to wait in a camp outside Monterrey, as the U.S. government sent supplies and more troops.

By September 21, when Taylor was ready to assault the city, the Mexicans had dug in for a last stand. Reinforcements swelled Taylor's ranks to 6,000 troops. But more than 9,000 Mexican soldiers awaited him behind the Monterrey walls.[11]

▽ Taylor assaulted the walled city of Monterrey and killed 4,000 Mexicans, many of them civilians.

Almost instantly, Taylor's forces found that the light artillery **guerrilla** attacks that had been so successful in Palo Alto were useless in Monterrey. U.S. soldiers had never engaged in this kind of city warfare before. As they marched through open city streets, Mexican fighters, hiding behind Monterrey's **adobe** homes, opened fire. Eleven West Point graduates—Taylor's finest soldiers—were cut down on the first day.

Two days later, Taylor changed his tactics. His men conducted house-to-house raids. Using picks and crowbars, they punched "mouse holes" into the adobe walls and fired 6-pound (2.7-kilogram) shells inside.[12] Often U.S. soldiers stormed through houses and fought hand-to-hand against the Mexican soldiers. As the Mexicans poured into the city's central plaza, Taylor's cannons overwhelmed them with firepower. Only 120 Americans were killed. Nearly 400 Mexicans died, including numerous civilians.

TAYLOR FOR PRESIDENT!

Taylor struck a deal with Ampudia. He knew that further fighting would result in more U.S. casualties. In return for the city's surrender, Taylor promised the Mexicans an eight-week truce. He also allowed the Mexican army to leave Monterrey. Over three days, the survivors marched from the walled city with their guns and uniforms.

Back in Washington, D.C., President Polk was furious. Taylor's job was to "kill the enemy"—not to allow them to escape with their weapons. Taylor countered that his own men needed time to regroup. He had dealt a severe blow to the Mexican army. After defending their well-fortified city for three days, Ampudia's 10,000 soldiers were no match for the smaller U.S. force. Their surrender, Taylor maintained, was demoralizing.[13]

But Polk was already thinking about whether he should replace Taylor. Back home, the general was becoming wildly popular. Writers had produced a New York stage show called "The Triumph of Rough and Ready." The Whig Party was mentioning Taylor as a candidate for president. To Polk, Taylor (a Whig) was a dangerous rival to his Democratic Party's hold on the presidency.

But there was one more battle for Taylor to win. And it would turn out to be the bloodiest of all.

A SOLDIER'S STORY

Lieutenant Daniel Harvey Hill ducked beneath a torn canvas tent and watched the rain pour over the campgrounds. As a member of the 4th Artillery, he had just helped General Zachary Taylor capture the Mexican town of Monterrey.

Hill, then 25, was tired and wet. And he was finding out the hard way that life in the U.S. Army in the 1840s was far from glamorous. "Two thirds of the tents furnished the army . . . were worn out and rotten," he wrote in an 1846 article describing army camp life. "Transparent as gauze, they afforded little or no protection against the intense heat of the summer, or the drenching rains and severe cold of winter."[14]

Lt. Daniel Harvey Hill later served as a Confederate general in the Civil War, participating in the Battle of Antietam (pictured).

HARDSHIPS DURING WAR

A South Carolina descendent of Irish immigrants, Hill was a studious and religious young man. He graduated from the West Point military academy and wanted to be a lifelong soldier. The Mexican campaign was his first experience with war. And he was discovering that the flag-waving parties back home had not prepared him for reality on the battlefield.

Like other soldiers, Hill endured many more hardships than enemy bullets. Many of the troops were in their teens and twenties. Most had never been away from home before. They enlisted for glory and adventure—but they found heat, dust, insects, and even death.

The food was bad, usually just slabs of beef or pork with hard bread. The canvas tents were cramped and ripped. And the rain never seemed to stop. "For days and weeks, every article in hundreds of tents were thoroughly soaked," Hill recalled.[15]

The threat of illness hung over the camp. The men used the river water of the Rio Grande for drinking, cooking, and bathing. Deadly diseases spread through the troops: **yellow fever**, **malaria**, **dysentery**, **smallpox**, and measles. Nearly 13 percent of the entire U.S. fight force was killed by disease. For every man cut down by a Mexican musket, seven more died from disease (see the chart on page 60).

Hill would go on to serve as a Confederate general in the Civil War. But the horrible sights he witnessed in Mexico would stay with him forever. As he sat in the rain, he recalled hearing wounded soldiers cry out in agony. "Their last groans mingled in fearful concert with the howling of the pitiless storm."[16]

TAYLOR ON THE MOVE

Taylor had declared a two-month cease-fire—and President Polk wasn't happy. Already suspicious of Taylor as a rival to his Democratic Party, now Polk felt that his general seemed to be deciding the conduct of the war. That was the president's job.

An angry Polk stripped Taylor of his ranks. Most of his army was sent to the Gulf Coast in preparation for an invasion of Mexico City. Taylor was told to stay put in Monterrey. But Taylor ignored the president's orders. With the 4,500 soldiers he had left, he marched deeper into Mexico.

Taylor was not the only soldier on the move. Mexico's Santa Anna (see box) had suddenly reentered the drama. After his humiliating defeat at the Battle of San Jacinto in 1836, which resulted in Mexico's loss of Texas, Santa Anna had fled to Cuba. From there, he wrote to the new Mexican government. He promised that he no longer wanted to be president. But he volunteered to help fight off the U.S. invaders.

BIOGRAPHY

General Antonio López de Santa Anna
1794–1876

BORN: Jalapa, Mexico

ROLE: Mexican general and president

Mexico's most famous general, the fiery and charismatic General Antonio López de Santa Anna at times served as the country's president and its military leader—or both. Still, he suffered humiliating defeat, losing the battle for Texas independence.

△ Santa Anna (pictured right) in full military dress.
Even after his 1836 loss to the Texas insurgents,
many Mexicans still saw Santa Anna as their savior.

At the same time, Santa Anna was also secretly negotiating with the United States. Polk had ordered a naval **blockade** along Mexico's east coast. Santa Anna asked the U.S. president to lift the blockade long enough for the Mexican general to sneak back into his country. Once he was back, Santa Anna vowed to stop the war and sell the disputed territories to Polk.

But Santa Anna was actually double-crossing both sides. In the summer of 1846, he slipped through the blockade and returned to Mexico. Immediately, he took control of the army, declared himself president, and once again rode into battle against the Americans.

Santa Anna was a savvy politician and a master *caudillo*, or military strongman. Despite his loss to the Texas insurgents in 1836, many Mexicans continued to see him as the nation's savior. If anyone could defeat the Americans and restore national honor, many believed it would be Santa Anna.[17]

U.S. WEAPONS OF WAR

U.S. soldiers had one huge advantage over their Mexican counterparts: their weapons. Most Americans were armed with rifles and muskets. The muskets were quick and easy to load, but they had limited range and accuracy. Others carried pistols, bayonets, and swords.[18] Some volunteers—particularly the Texas recruits—were notorious for arming themselves with as many weapons as possible. They had pistols, knives, and revolvers tucked into their boots, belts, and shirts.

The things they carried

U.S. soldiers had to travel light. From battle to battle, they plodded through the heat and dust of the Mexican chaparral. Every ounce of extra weight made the hot sun and thick bush harder to navigate. Volunteers, like the Texan regiment, might carry a variety of knives and pistols. But most soldiers had about 30 pounds (14 kilograms) of gear—including a 9.5-pound (4.3-kilogram) musket, ammunition, a bayonet, a canteen of water, a blanket, and a haversack (a shoulder strap bag) with food and small personal items.

The United States won the war's arms race thanks in part to its artillery—its heavy guns. U.S. troops had cannonballs, shells, and canisters that could fire lead balls and explosives as far as 300 yards (274 meters) into an enemy camp. The artillery was equipped with long-barreled cannons and rocket-like **mortars**. U.S. troops also had the latest rifles. Later in the war, the cavalry was issued 1,000 brand-new Colt revolvers, the most accurate and fastest-loading guns of their time.

MEXICAN WEAPONRY

Mexican weaponry was older, heavier, and less reliable. The average Mexican infantryman carried an old flintlock musket called a Brown Bess. Most were made by the British, who had long since dismissed the weapons as outdated. The guns were of such poor quality that their heavy lead balls often jammed in the barrel.[19]

In the wake of one battle, U.S. solider George Ballentine came across dozens of discarded muskets and bayonets left behind by retreating Mexicans troops. "They were old and worn out, having evidently been condemned as unserviceable in the British army and then sold to the Mexicans at a low price," Ballentine wrote. "After examining a few of them I came to the conclusion that for efficient service one of our muskets was equal to at least three of them."[20]

The old guns also forced Mexican soldiers to adopt an unusual shooting style. Their cumbersome muskets used too much heavy powder. Many Mexican soldiers could not even raise the rifles up to their shoulders. Instead, they fired from the hip. As a result, their shots often sailed over the heads of their targets. U.S. soldiers used a more accurate method. They butted the rifle up to their shoulders and took aim along the barrel.[21]

△ American soldiers were better equipped for war than their Mexican counterparts. U.S. troops had the newest guns and weapons while Mexican soldados had old heavy muskets.

SANTA ANNA MARCHES NORTH

After Monterrey fell (see pages 28 and 29), Santa Anna raised a massive army of 20,000 soldados. His spies intercepted a letter to Taylor, revealing that the general's forces had been reduced. Now was the time to act.

In February 1847, Santa Anna quickly marched north to intercept Taylor's increasingly small army.[22] The march was difficult on Santa Anna. He led his men on a grueling hike through deserts and over mountains, with almost no food or water. By the time he encountered Taylor's forces, many of his army had **deserted**.[23]

THE BATTLE OF BUENA VISTA

Taylor was entrenched in a mountain pass called Buena Vista, in what is now northern Mexico. Despite the Mexican desertions, Taylor was still vastly outnumbered by Santa Anna's army. Over the course of two days, the armies waged a furious fight. The Battle of Buena Vista was the single bloodiest battle of the war.

With Mexicans surrounding the U.S. forces, it appeared Santa Anna had the upper hand. He demanded Taylor's surrender on February 22. The U.S. general refused. The next morning, Santa Anna ordered an all-out assault. He broke through the U.S. line by midday.

But Taylor's troops were backed by a legion of Mississippi volunteer soldiers. They were led by Colonel Jefferson Davis (who would later serve as the president of the Confederacy during the Civil War). Although Davis was shot in the foot, his troops stalled Santa Anna's attack until Taylor's forces could regroup.[24]

"GIVE THEM HELL, BRAGG!"

As heavy rain violently drenched the battlefield, Taylor rode his horse, Old Whitey, through a hail of Mexican gunfire. He paused at an artillery battery led by Captain Braxton Bragg. Taylor ordered the soldier to hold his ground at any cost. "Give them hell, Bragg!" he shouted. (This would become Taylor's 1848 presidential campaign slogan.)[25]

The Mexicans had heavy losses. Nearly 600 of Santa Anna's troops were dead. Close to 300 Americans died while fighting on the rough mountain **terrain**. Santa Anna withdrew that night, leaving Taylor in control of northern Mexico.

△ The Battle of Buena Vista was the bloodiest contest of the war. Both sides suffered heavy losses. In the end, both the U.S. and Mexico claimed victory.

EXTRA! EXTRA!

George Wilkins Kendall witnessed the Mexican-American War firsthand. He was on the scene when Texas revolted against Mexico. And he had been alongside General Taylor at Palo Alto. He was even wounded in battle.[26] But Kendall wasn't a soldier. He was a reporter for the *New Orleans Picayune*. He wasn't on the battlefield to fight. He was getting a story.

Millions of readers back in the United States hung on Kendall's every word, eager for news from the front. But it was not easy to get his stories in print. As he dodged Mexican fire, Kendall scribbled on scraps of paper. Riders on horseback would carry his stories. If they made it to a Texas telegraph office, Kendall's words would travel over a wire to his Louisiana paper. Within weeks of Kendall witnessing a battle, Picayune readers would thrill to every detail.

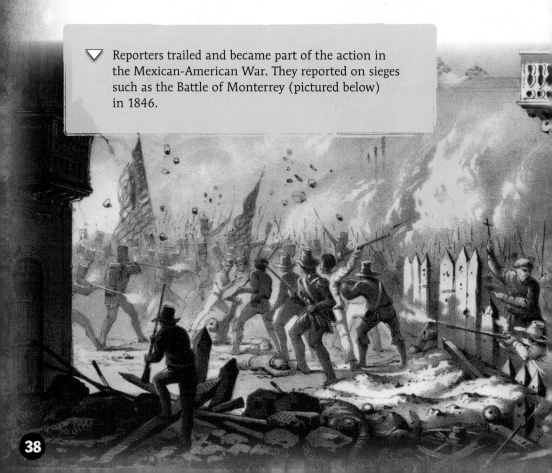

▽ Reporters trailed and became part of the action in the Mexican-American War. They reported on sieges such as the Battle of Monterrey (pictured below) in 1846.

The 1840s were a golden age of communication. Steam-powered printing presses and magnetic telegraphs relayed news faster than ever. Americans read in huge numbers, and their favorite subject was the war. They celebrated news of victories with firework displays and parades. War figures like General Zachary Taylor became national heroes, mythologized in Broadway musicals like "The Siege of Monterrey, or The Triumph of Rough and Ready." Readers devoured "pulp" novels with titles like *The Mexican Spy: or, The Bride of Buena Vista*.[27] Most of the books and shows were fun adventure stories. But for reporters like Kendall, the battles in Mexico were very real.

At the time, Kendall's cables were the closest thing to 24-hour news. He was among the first modern war correspondents—journalists on the battlefield. Kendall's stories shaped the public's views and attitudes about the war. For the first time in U.S. history, the public was getting its news about war from journalists in action, not politicians in Washington.

A DANGEROUS JOB

Newspapermen were so common among soldiers that 20 New Orleans reporters trailed one company. The press corps included Kendall and his main competitor, James L. Freaner of the Daily Delta. Freaner was nicknamed "Mustang." He had earned the name during the Battle of Monterrey, when he stabbed a Mexican soldier with a lance (a steel-tipped spear)—and rode off on his horse![28]

Kendall and Freaner were determined to be the first journalists with war news. But as they followed troops over mountains and through dense jungles, it became harder to get their reports back to the home front. Mexican soldiers and armed bandits roamed the countryside. The reporters' horse-riding messengers were often robbed or killed. At one time, Kendall and Freaner each sent five different messengers with stories—and none of them got through. One of Freaner's riders was found hung by his neck to a tree. His murderers pinned a sign to his chest reading "Correo de los Yankees" ("Yankee Messenger").[29]

Five bandits attacked one of Kendall's riders. They stabbed him repeatedly and tore Kendall's handwritten news report to bits. Remarkably, the rider lived—and delivered the paper scraps to his editors in New Orleans![30]

In all, Kendall filed 214 reports, and he became the best-known correspondent of the war.

GO WEST!

The West was a 2,000-mile (3,220-kilometer) stretch of land from the Mississippi River to the Rocky Mountains. Future western states—Arizona, California, Colorado, Nevada, New Mexico, Texas, and Utah—had been under Spanish control there since the 16th century.

Even after Mexico seized the land in 1821, Americans rarely ventured to the West. By 1830 fewer than 100,000 settlers had even crossed the Mississippi River.[1] The few Americans who had ventured there were explorers, fur trappers, traders, and **missionaries**.[2]

PARADISE?

By the 1840s, Americans knew very little about the western half of their continent. They had heard California described as a lush, green paradise. But they had also heard tales of a life-threatening journey.

It would take travelers five months to drive a covered wagon from Missouri to California. Along the way, pioneers and their families would brave vast expanses of sun-baked grasslands, which were treeless and waterless. They feared that American Indian tribes like the Sauk and the Pottawatomi were waiting to "scalp" (removed the scalp of) careless travelers.[3] There were mountains like the Rockies and the Sierra Nevada that made crossing difficult.

Manifest Destiny–minded adventurers believed they should own all the land up to the Pacific. But, at this point, the West did not actually belong to the United States. It was part of Mexico.

President Polk wanted the West. Great Britain also wanted Oregon, but Polk was desperate to block a British presence on the continent. Polk had tried to buy the western territories in the same secret mission that sent Slidell to Mexico City (see page 17). He had also dispatched representatives to both Monterey, California, and Santa Fe, in present-day New Mexico. He assured the settlers there that they would have U.S. support if they chose to "play the Texas game," as California settlers called it, and break from Mexico.[4]

California

What was California like during the time of the Mexican-American War? The total population was about 6,000 Mexicans and local American Indians. Mexican cattle ranchers roamed the remote landscape. Only about 800 Americans lived there.

Mexico had left California practically ungoverned. It was far from the central government in Mexico City. The few people who lived in the West often did not consider themselves Mexican or American. President Polk needed the support of these people if he was going to succeed in making California a part of the United States.

President James K. Polk desperately wanted the West for the United States and sought to block the British from their expansion plans.

"NOTHING TO LOSE"

Beginning in the 1840s, Americans embarked on a great western expansion, fleeing the crowded East for the West's wide-open spaces. Between 1841 and 1867, more than 350,000 people traveled west along overland trails. They were seeking better lives and relief from an economic depression that gripped much of the United States in the late 1830s. Others had seen their homes and lives destroyed by floods and disease in the Mississippi Valley. Whatever waited for them out west couldn't be any worse. As one pioneer woman said: "We had nothing to lose, and we might gain a fortune."[5]

Many pioneers were tempted by the promise of rich, fertile California land. As they trekked westward, families chalked "California or Bust" on their wagons. In 1846 alone, 2,700 people headed west, with 1,500 aiming for California. When gold was discovered in California in 1848, more people journeyed west for a prosperous new life.

The Oregon Trail

Between 1845 and 1859, nearly 300,000 travelers embarked on the famous Oregon Trail—a 2,000-mile (3,220-kilometer) east-to-west wagon route. The trail linked towns along the Missouri River to valleys in Oregon. But the trip was hazardous and often deadly. Although estimates vary, at least 20,000 would die on the Oregon Trail.[6]

HARD JOURNEY

Every spring, pioneers gathered at way stations like Independence, Missouri, and Council Bluffs, Iowa, to begin the approximately 2,000-mile (3,220-kilometer) journey. Most traveled with their entire families, including many infant children. They drove covered wagons pulled by oxen or horses. The men carried rifles, shotguns, and even brand-new Samuel Colt revolvers. Their supplies included flour, bacon, salt, sugar, coffee, rice, and bread or tough flour-and-water biscuits called hardtack. Preparing for the journey cost as much as $1,500. It was such an enormous sum that many families sold off their land and livestock to gather the cash.[7]

Along the route, men drove the wagons and tended the animals. They stood guard duty and hunted buffalo and antelope. Women got up at four in the morning and collected wood and "buffalo chips" (animal dung) for campfires. They hauled water, kneaded dough, and milked cows—along with preparing meals, washing clothes, and looking after the children.[8]

Accidents, disease, and sudden disaster were ever-present dangers. Children fell out of wagons. Women died in childbirth. The oxen dropped dead from hauling the immense wagons. Illnesses like **typhoid**, dysentery, and **mountain fever** threatened pioneers. The settlers were not careful with their latrines (toilets dug in the ground) and garbage. They left their waste across the landscape, spreading diseases like **cholera** to the families that followed behind them. Others died from buffalo stampedes, fires, floods, and rare attacks by American Indians.[9] Traveling west was as dangerous as going to war. Indeed, when it came to conquering California, settlers would be as important as soldiers.

▽ It was "California or Bust" for many of the settlers who boarded covered wagons and headed west in 1846, searching for prosperity and better lives.

DEATH ON THE JOURNEY WEST

In the spring of 1846, Charles Stanton, a single 35-year-old man, set out for a new life in the American West. He hoped to find prosperity and adventure. Along the way, he wrote to his brother, "I have seen the Rocky Mountains...am now on the waters that flow to the Pacific! It seems as if I had left the old world behind and a new one is dawning upon me."[10]

But Stanton's new life would turn out to be short-lived. Stanton was traveling with an ill-fated group of pioneers known as the Donner party. The 87 men, women, and children were heading to the West—but only half would make it there alive.[11]

In April 1846, the party left Springfield, Illinois, for California. They were led by George Donner, a wealthy 62-year-old farmer. The western route was so dangerous that pioneers often combined parties and traveled in packs. Stanton, a Chicago businessman, joined the Donner party in Wyoming.

The travelers were poorly prepared for the dangerous journey. Their 27 wagons were weighed down with fancy foods and liquor and cumbersome beds and stoves.[12] In July, as the party left Wyoming, they took a shortcut. The path was recommended in a guidebook by a famous explorer. But the author had never actually taken the new route. He claimed it would cut 400 miles (644 kilometers) off the journey. Instead, it led the party to its doom.

Soon, huge boulders, dry deserts, and dangerous mountain passes slowed the expedition to a crawl. The wagons covered just 36 miles (58 kilometers) in 21 days. The book said one deadly hot desert crossing would take two days. Instead, it lasted six days and nights. With supplies running low, Stanton volunteered to take a dangerous journey to retrieve more food from a frontier trading post. He cut through dangerous canyons and sidestepped falling boulders. But he returned, carting seven mules with supplies.[13]

TRAPPED IN THE MOUNTAINS

The Donner party had been on the frontier passage for months. They neared their destination, California's Sacramento Valley. Stanton and the rest of the party merely had to cross the Sierra Nevada Mountains. But in late October, as they climbed the high ridges toward their final pass, a fierce blizzard blew through the mountains. The party's path was blocked by 5–10 feet (1.5–3 meters) of snow.

Trapped, the pioneers wrapped themselves in tents, blankets, and animal hides. They were forced to eat mice, rugs, and even their own shoes. Finally, with no food left and pinned down by severe storms, they were forced to eat the flesh of those who had died.

A month later, seven survivors, delirious and frostbitten, reached a U.S. camp. It took four attempts for rescue parties to find the others.[14] Only 47 of the 87 Donner party pioneers lived through the ordeal.

Stanton was not one of them. In December 1846, after helping other travelers cross the Sierra Nevada, Stanton was too weak to continue. Snow-blind and frozen, he told his companions to go on without him. Lighting his pipe in the snow, he promised he would follow behind. His body was found in the same spot a year later.[15]

△ The doomed Donner party headed west in 1846. Beset by storms and rough terrain, only 47 of the party's 87 men, women, and children survived.

FRÉMONT

In the winter of 1846, a rugged adventurer wandered out of the cold and into the California history books. John C. Frémont (see box) was a military officer. But he was best known as the most famous explorer in the United States.

Frémont was leading a group of 55 men on a mission to locate the source of the Arkansas River. But he abruptly handed the expedition over to another explorer. The famed Frémont said he had business in California. Months later, Frémont arrived in Monterey, California, with a pack of 60 heavily armed men.

A Mexican general was in charge of what was then called Upper California. The general was concerned. What could this famous U.S. explorer want? And why was he traveling with a band of **roughnecks**?

That question is still debated today. Frémont insisted he was merely stopping in Monterey for supplies on his way to Oregon. To others, he claimed to be scouting out a seaside home for his mother.

But some believe Frémont was acting on secret orders from President Polk himself. His mission, many think, was to stir up trouble in California—to incite U.S. settlers to revolt against the Mexican authorities.[16]

THE BEAR FLAG REVOLT

The suspicious Mexican general soon chased Frémont from Monterey. The explorer retreated to Oregon. But he returned in June. On June 15, 1846, 30 settlers, mostly U.S. citizens, seized the small Mexican town of Sonoma. At the time, word had not reached the West that the United States and Mexico were at war. The rebels hoisted a homemade flag painted with a crude likeness of a grizzly bear and the words "California Republic." Like Texas, California was declaring its independence.

△ Today, California's state flag still resembled the original "Bear Flag" that rebelling settlers hoisted in 1846.

But unlike the struggle in Texas, "the Bear Flag Revolt" was largely bloodless. It was also temporary. Just a week after the band of rebels declared California independent, the U.S. Army, led by Frémont, took over. As U.S. Navy ships docked in Pacific ports, town after California town was taken without resistance, from Sonoma to San Francisco. On August 13, 1846, 50 marines walked into Los Angeles and declared the city conquered— without ever firing a shot.

Did you know?

After the war, Frémont served as a senator from California. In 1856 the Great Pathfinder became the first Republican candidate for president, losing to James Buchanan. He also fought in the Union Army during the Civil War.

ACROSS THE WEST

As General Zachary Taylor scored victories in northern Mexico, another part of the U.S. Army was also on the move. In the summer of 1846 the "Army of the West," commanded by General Stephen Kearny (see box), had two goals: to conquer the territory of New Mexico and to continue on to California.

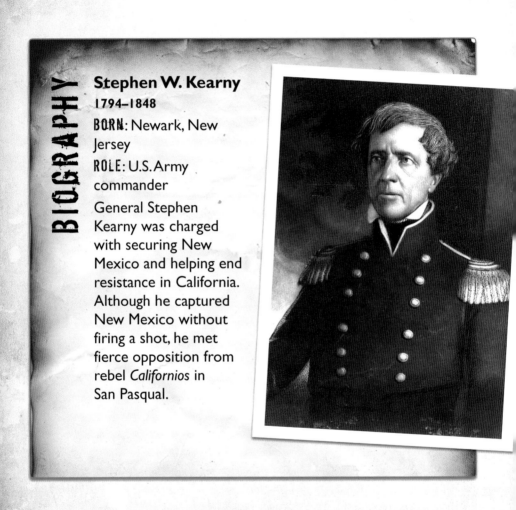

BIOGRAPHY

Stephen W. Kearny
1794–1848
BORN: Newark, New Jersey
ROLE: U.S. Army commander
General Stephen Kearny was charged with securing New Mexico and helping end resistance in California. Although he captured New Mexico without firing a shot, he met fierce opposition from rebel *Californios* in San Pasqual.

With 2,500 men—more than 1,000 of whom were volunteers—Kearny marched west into the "Great American Desert." It was a grueling trip. His army trekked more than 1,000 miles (1,600 kilometers) in two months. Kearny's men had never been deep in the West. They marveled as they marched passed herds of bison (buffalo). Along the way, Kearny prepared for a fight. He anticipated fierce resistance in Santa Fe.

Kearny was wrong. New Mexico was captured without a fight, in mid-August. The territory had 80,000 inhabitants. They had grown wealthy by trading goods with the United States. Joining the Union, they believed, could only increase their fortune. They looked forward to becoming U.S. citizens.[17]

CALIFORNIOS

With New Mexico settled, Kearny set out for California. Along the way, scouts informed him that California was already in U.S. hands. Still, Kearny pressed on. With 300 mounted soldiers, Kearny crossed 850 miles (1,368 kilometers) through the territories of New Mexico, Arizona, and the Sonora Desert. Tired, dirty, and exhausted, Kearny arrived at an Indian village near San Diego called San Pasqual—and found the first real resistance to U.S. troops in the West.

The resistors were called *Californios*—Californians of Latin American descent. Some were the sons of agricultural settlers and Mexican soldiers. Others were **mestizos**. And they were not about to let their land be taken without a fight.

Kearny finally had his battle. The *Californio* lancers were fierce and well trained. Kearny's own men were drained from their hike across the desert. In a driving rainstorm, Kearny ordered an early-morning attack. He was hoping for a swift victory. But the lancers easily defeated the Americans—partly because the downpour soaked the Americans' gunpowder. With 17 of his soldiers killed, Kearny retreated to San Diego.

> ### Did you know?
> Kearny and Frémont argued over who should be the governor of the newly conquered western lands. Their bickering became so bad that Kearny had Frémont arrested and court-martialed. Just a year after the war, Kearny contracted malaria and died.[18]

In January 1847, Kearny met with U.S. Navy Commodore Robert F. Stockton outside Los Angeles. *Californio* forces had mounted an attack and seized the city from Frémont. With a joint Army–Navy assault, Kearny and Stockton finally suppressed the *Californio* uprising. The entire western territory was now under U.S. control.

THE FALL OF MEXICO

Northern Mexico and the West had fallen. It seemed a matter of time before the United States could claim total victory. By the end of 1847, President Polk prepared for a final assault. In order to end the war, he believed, his army would have to capture Mexico's capital, Mexico City.

GENERAL SCOTT'S PLAN

Polk would not hand the job to Zachary Taylor. The general had scored numerous victories and was wildly popular among both the troops and the public. But "Old Rough and Ready" was Polk's political rival. The antislavery Whigs were even mentioning Taylor's name as a possible presidential candidate.[1]

Instead, Polk appointed a new commander. His name was General Winfield Scott (see box). In many ways, he was Taylor's opposite. While Taylor was known for his straw hat and his bond with his men, Scott was a stickler for detail, discipline, and strict military appearance. But like Taylor, Scott was a fearless, battle-hardened veteran. He had led soldiers in the War of 1812 and won battles against the Seminole Indians and the Cherokees in Georgia.

Scott proposed a bold plan: He would invade Mexico by sea. He would land a massive army on the eastern beaches along the Gulf of Mexico, near the Mexican city of Veracruz. Then he would march overland to capture Mexico City—following the same route Hernán Cortés had taken when he conquered the Aztecs 300 years before.[2]

Polk was skeptical. It would require the greatest naval landing in history. No one had ever attempted such an ambitious **amphibious** assault.

Did you know?

A large and imposing figure, as a young man Scott was 6 feet, 5 inches (196 centimeters) tall and weighed 230 pounds (104 kilograms). By the time he lost the presidential election to Pierce, Scott is reported to have weighed over 300 pounds (136 kilograms).[3]

THE BATTLE OF VERACRUZ

In the early morning of March 9, 1847, shiploads of U.S. soldiers rowed ashore in specially built surfboats. By nightfall, 12,000 soldiers—with supplies, weapons, and even horses—waded to the Gulf beach. It was the first major amphibious landing in U.S. history. Among Scott's invading force were several soldiers who would become famous in the Civil War, including Robert E. Lee, Thomas "Stonewall" Jackson, and Ulysses S. Grant.[4]

The troops landed in the shadow of Veracruz, an imposing city surrounded by towering stone walls. About 3,400 men were in place to defend the city. Scott's troops surrounded Veracruz as U.S. Navy ships shelled its walls from the coast. For three weeks, the city was overwhelmed by a constant bombardment. Mexican officials pleaded with Scott to allow women and children to leave the city. Scott refused. Mortars pounded the mighty stone walls.

Finally, on March 29, 1847, with more than 700 dead—including 400 civilians—the Mexican forces surrendered. In the face of the relentless U.S. attack, the impenetrable walls of Veracruz finally fell.

THE MARCH TO THE CAPITAL

After his stunning naval landing at Veracruz, General Scott marched his army of 10,000 men toward his ultimate goal: the capital, Mexico City. He met little resistance along the way. Many villagers allowed Americans to pass through peacefully. Mexican soldiers deserted their army in large numbers. Santa Anna's depleted forces could barely withstand another U.S. assault.

A Mexican solider

Ramón Alacaraz, an officer in the Mexican army, fought under General Santa Anna. He wrote a book about his experiences, entitled *The Other Side: Or Notes for the History of the War Between Mexico and the United States*. In the book, he described the fighting at Cerro Gordo:

Horrible, indeed, was the descent by that narrow and rocky path, where thousands rushed . . . leaving a track of blood upon the road. . . .The enemy, now masters of our camp, turned their guns upon the fugitives. This augmented [increased] more and more the terror of the multitude.[5]

As Mexican soldiers fled and their leaders chased after them, "Cerro-Gordo was lost!" Alacaraz reported. "Mexico was open to the iniquity [unjust behavior] of the invader."[6]

Alacaraz also wrote about the life of the average Mexican soldier, which was dreary and deadly. Their food was so scarce that they scrounged for supplies as they marched through local villages. Most *soldados* feared their own officers more than the enemy. The officer corps was made up of wealthy aristocrats. The soldiers were landless peasants, mestizos, or Indians. The officers had almost no regard for the life of their men. Santa Anna referred to his soldiers as "mere chickens."[7] Some Mexican officers slashed at their men with sabers. Others stole from their own troops.[8]

About 50 miles (80 kilometers) inland, Santa Anna mustered as many troops as he could find to intercept the unstoppable U.S. advance. Scott's men were headed toward a mountain pass called Cerro Gordo. Santa Anna planned to block their path. With 12,000 *soldados*, he waited for the Americans.[9]

AMBUSH

Scott knew his men were marching into an ambush. Mexican guns were aimed at the mountain road—and Scott saw no way around them. But then Captain Robert E. Lee had a plan. Lee had just returned from a scouting mission. Sketching a crude map of the mountain pass, he showed Scott how to outflank the Mexican ambush.

On April 18, Lee led his soldiers through muddy terrain around the pass.[10] The men struggled with the rough passage, but they found high ground above Santa Anna's forces. Surrounded, the Mexican army was defeated. The United States suffered over 350 casualties, but Mexico lost more than 1,000 men in the mountain pass battle. The Mexicans fled so quickly that they left behind piles of supplies—weapons, food, uniforms, and even Santa Anna's spare wooden leg.[12]

Deserters

Americans also saw their fair share of runaways. The squalid Mexican front and the miserable conditions in camp caused more than 8 percent of U.S. soldiers to flee. A few hundred deserters even switched sides. Nearly all were recent immigrants from Europe who had sympathy with Mexico's Spanish and Catholic heritage (see pages 54 and 55).[11]

Santa Anna's troops were ragged and exhausted. They had fought valiantly, but they had suffered defeat after defeat. Some secretly snuck away in the middle of the night. But others fought on—even though their cause seemed hopelessly lost.

THE SAINT PATRICK'S BATTALION

On the morning of September 10, 1847, 16 U.S. soldiers were marched through the Mexican town of San Angel.[13] Their hands were tied behind their backs and their heads were bowed. They were led to the **gallows**, where 16 swinging nooses awaited them. The men had been court-martialed by the U.S. army. Their charge was treason. They had been found guilty and sentenced to death by hanging.

The condemned men were members of the Saint Patrick's Battalion— the *San Patricios*, as Mexicans called them. Mostly Irish immigrants, they had served with the U.S. Army. But they had all deserted and switched sides. They fought for Mexico against the United States. To this day, Americans consider them traitors. But Mexicans revere them as heroes.

IRISH IMMIGRANTS

Between 1820 and 1930, 4.5 million Irish immigrated to the United States. In the 1840s, as Ireland suffered from a massive famine (lack of food), almost half of U.S. immigrants were Irish. Most were Catholic, and many spoke only Gaelic. Thousands volunteered for the war. With monthly earnings of $7, the Army seemed like a good living for poor immigrants.[14]

Still, the U.S.-born Protestant commanders often treated the Irish as half-human. Some officers refused to let the displaced Catholics hold their religious service, Sunday mass. With only loose ties to the United States, Irish immigrants began wondering what they were fighting for.

At the same time, Mexico encouraged the immigrants to desert the U.S. Army and fight alongside their Catholic brothers. Mexican soldiers littered battlefields with letters addressed to foreign-born U.S. soldiers. They promised 320 acres (129 hectares) of free land if they crossed the Rio Grande for a new home in Mexico.

JOHN RILEY

The most famous deserter—and founder of the battalion—was John Riley. A native of Ireland's Galway, Riley had served with the British army in Canada, before jumping the border to the United States. He fought with Zachary Taylor on the Rio Grande. But he also saw roughneck U.S. volunteers burn down a Mexican farm village (see page 57). The Irish soldier began to wonder if he was fighting on the wrong side.[15]

One morning, Riley's commander gave him permission to cross into Mexico to attend a Catholic mass. Riley took the opportunity to join the Mexican army. With his second-in-command, Patrick Dalton, Riley persuaded 48 other Irishmen to desert. They formed the core of the original *San Patricios*. Eventually, their ranks would swell to more than 200, including Germans and other Catholic immigrants.[16]

The battalion had a reputation as ruthless fighters. Near the end of the war, while U.S. troops overran the Mexican city of Churubusco, the *San Patricios* refused to surrender. When one Mexican soldier raised a white flag in defeat, Dalton shot him dead. Santa Anna would later proclaim that if he had more men like the *San Patricios*, Mexico would have won the war.[17]

D FOR "DESERTER"

After Mexico's defeat, most of the *San Patricios* were captured. Many were set free and returned to Ireland. As a punishment for desertion, some received whip lashes. According to a U.S. eyewitness, "Their backs had the appearance of a pounded piece of raw beef, the blood oozing from every stripe."[18] After the flogging, the prisoners were branded (burned) with the letter D—for "deserter." Riley had the mark branded on both cheeks with red-hot irons.

Riley was spared the noose. But about half the soldiers, including Dalton, were sentenced to die.[19]

VOLUNTEERS FOR WAR

At the outbreak of war, the U.S. Army consisted of fewer than 9,000 professional soldiers—not nearly enough to fight Mexico. The rest of the fighting force was made up of volunteers. These included more than 50,000 men with almost no training and, in some cases, no discipline.

The volunteers were assigned by states. Texas, Louisiana, or Arkansas volunteers, for example, made up individual units. Most volunteers proved their courage as combat soldiers. But members of the Army shunned other volunteers as poor soldiers. One troop of Louisiana volunteers arrived to help Taylor capture the walled city of Monterrey. Dubbed "Gaines's Army" after the general who recruited them, the volunteers were so incompetent that Taylor sent them home. (Today, the expression "Just like Gaines's Army" refers to something useless.[20])

In some cases, the volunteers weren't just bad soldiers. They were also ruthless and bloodthirsty. John Riley of the San Patricios may have been inspired to desert after seeing a volunteer company burn down a Mexican farm village. Back in Washington, D.C., Congressman Abraham Lincoln harshly rebuked the badly behaved volunteers for this action. He said:

> It is a fact that the United States army . . . marched into a peaceful Mexican settlement and frightened the inhabitants away from their homes and their growing crops. . . Possibly you consider these acts too small for notice. Would you venture to so consider them so had they been committed by any nation on earth against the humblest of our people?[21]

Worst of all were a wild regiment of Arkansas volunteers known as the Rackensackers (see box on page 57). While serving under Taylor's command, the Rackensackers heard of a rumor about a Mexican man who had killed a U.S. soldier for insulting a woman. They took their revenge with a bloody massacre. The Rackensackers rounded up 20 Mexican men, women, and children hiding in a nearby cave. The volunteers slaughtered them all. No one was punished for the crime.

This 1846 poster depicts the inexperience of American volunteers for the war. The uniformed officer faces civilians (one carrying a parasol).

DUTY IS FINISHED

Winfield Scott had the Mexican army in a vulnerable position. After his victories at Veracruz and Cerro Gordo, nothing could stop his march to Mexico City—and the capital's fall.

Nothing could stop him, that is, except his own army. As Scott's forces set up camp, hundreds of his men abruptly left for home. They were not deserters. They were volunteers. They had signed on for 12 months of duty. Now their service was up, and they were being shipped back to the United States. Scott had no choice but to wait for a new batch of volunteers to arrive.

Rackensacker Massacre

In his memoir, U.S. soldier Samuel Chamberlain described the scene he found as his Army unit reached the cave where the Rackensacker Massacre took place:

Shouts and curses, cries of women and children, reached our ears, coming from a cave… We reached the entrance and as soon as we could see in the … darkness a horrid sight was before us. The cave was full of our volunteers yelling like fiends, while on the rocky floor lay over twenty Mexicans, dead and dying in pools of blood. Women and children were clinging to the knees of the murderers and shrieking for mercy.[22]

THE SCOURGE OF YELLOW FEVER

General Scott anxiously awaited new troops. After his stirring victories, Mexican soldiers were becoming demoralized. Scott was eager to march toward Mexico City without delay.

But Scott's worries had little do to with Santa Anna's troops. He was in a desperate race against a killer disease. And the longer he waited, the more of his men it claimed.[23] The disease was called yellow fever—or, as the Mexicans knew it, *La Vomito*. It caused headaches, fever, chills, and vomiting. Its victims' skin turned yellow as their livers failed. The sick soldiers' arteries and veins burst open as their lungs filled with blood.

Yellow fever frightened Scott more than the Mexicans. He knew he could defeat Santa Anna. But there was no cure for yellow fever. A fifth of the soldiers who developed it were doomed to die. If he could not reach Mexico City before the disease reached its deadly peak in the spring, the disease might wipe out most of his army.[24]

OTHER DEADLY DISEASES

Scott knew that yellow fever season started in the spring. He planned many of his attacks, including the naval assault on Veracruz, to avoid the disease. But the delays, as he waited for troop and supplies, ruined his plans. Yellow fever struck some of his troops as soon as they landed on the Mexican beach.

Did you know?

At the time of the Mexican-American War, doctors did not know how to treat yellow fever or understand what caused it. Later, they would learn that the disease was transmitted to people through mosquito bites. The moist Mexican jungles were a perfect breeding ground for the mosquitoes that carried yellow fever. And there was nothing the 19th-century U.S. soldier could do to protect himself from their bites.

Yellow fever was not just a problem during wartime. Between 1693 and 1901, 95 separate yellow fever epidemics ravaged the United States. It killed 100,000 people in cities like Philadelphia, Boston, New York, and New Orleans.[25]

But, overall, Scott was lucky. His troops never suffered from a major outbreak of yellow fever. Other diseases were more deadly. The poor sanitation at the Army camps led to outbreaks of diarrhea, dysentery, and typhoid. These and other disease, including measles, smallpox, and cholera, killed more people than enemy gunfire.

At Veracruz, General Scott pulled off the first major amphibious landing in U.S. history. General Scott planned many of his attacks to avoid the problem of yellow fever.

ADVANCE ON THE CAPITAL

By August 1847, General Scott had new troops. He was ready to move on to Mexico City. But the delay had also given Santa Anna enough time to recuperate from his loss at Cerro Gordo.

Scott approached Mexico City from the southwest. It was the muddiest path, but also the least defended. Scott's men hiked over lava beds and rough terrain. In a few days, even as more soldiers dropped from yellow fever, the U.S. advance was just 9 miles (14.5 kilometers) south of the capital.

But Scott soon met heavy fighting as his troops once again encountered Santa Anna's persistent army. The depleted Mexican forces fell back to the Mexican city of Churubusco. The general barricaded his troops in a heavily fortified convent (a religious residence for nuns).

As Santa Anna's men fired down on the surging Americans, Scott's artillery battered the convent until the Mexicans surrendered. In two battles, Mexico lost 10,000 Mexican men, while the Americans had 1,000 casualties. Santa Anna slipped away again, this time gathering his troop at a fortress called Chapultepec.

THE FINAL ASSAULT

Chapultepec was an imposing structure—a large castle-style fort, surrounded by a vast park and a high wall. Starting on September 12, the U.S. artillery pounded the Mexican castle for more than a day, until waves of soldiers stormed the walls.

U.S. casualties in the Mexican-American War

The following numbers show the total number of U.S. casualties in the Mexican-American War, from 1846 to 1848:

- Killed in action: 1,192
- Wounded: 529
- Deaths due to accidents: 362
- Deaths due to disease: 11,155

Note: Disease and wound deaths sometimes occurred after 1848.[26]

△ General's Scott's troops marched into Mexico City in September of 1846, unofficially ending the war.

Scott's forces triumphantly marched into the main plaza. A small force of U.S. Marines took over the National Palace and raised the U.S. flag. By the time Chapultepec fell on September 13, 2,000 Mexicans and 450 Americans were dead. Even today, a popular song celebrating the U.S. Marines refers to the "From the Halls of Montezuma" at the National Palace.[27]

U.S. troops entered Mexico City that afternoon. Shortly after midnight, Santa Anna evacuated his troops. On September 16, Santa Anna resigned as the Mexican president. He fled the country in October. The war was over.

Mexican casualties in the Mexican-American War

Reports of Mexican casualties in the Mexican-American War were extremely sketchy. Mexican officers sometimes held soldiers in low regard and didn't keep accurate statistics. Some sources say 25,000 soldiers were killed or wounded in action, but the number is probably higher.

LOS NIÑOS HÉROES

Juan Escutia stood on the roof of the mighty Chapultepec Castle. The Americans were about to overrun the stone fortress. Escutia was an artillery second lieutenant and one of the last surviving soldiers in his Mexican army unit. And Escutia was just 15 years old.

As the U.S. guns drew closer, Escutia wrapped himself in the Mexican flag. Balanced on the edge of the roof, he vowed to keep his country's flag out of the invaders' hands, even if he had to die for it. As Americans stormed toward him, he jumped from the roof—falling to his death.

△ The Monument to the Heroic Cadets in Chapultepec, Mexico, honors the teenage soldiers known as *Niños Héroes*.

Escutia was part of a famed legion of teen fighters known as *Los Niños Héroes* ("the Boy Heroes"). The six young soldiers, all between the ages of 13 and 19, defended the Chapultepec Castle from the U.S. invaders. Hopelessly outnumbered, they stood their ground until there was no choice but to surrender or die. Some of the six were killed by enemy fire. Others chose to commit suicide.[28] While historians question whether Escutia's story is completely accurate, Mexicans revere him for jumping from the castle roof to protect the Mexican flag.[29]

Juan de la Barrera, the oldest "*niño*" at 19, enlisted in the army at age 12. During the attack on Chapultepec, he was a lieutenant. He died defending a gun battery at the entrance to the castle grounds. Francisco Marquez, 13, was the youngest of the crew. His body was found on a hill near the castle, alongside the body of Escutia.[30]

"I RESPECT BRAVERY"

The six youths are buried in what is now called Chapultepec Park, in Mexico City. In 1952 the remains of all six *Niños Héroes* were moved under the Monument to the Heroic Cadets in Chapultepec. The cadets are honored by a series of large marble monuments, along with a large mural depicting Escutia's leap. Their names appear on streets, squares, and schools across the country. Their images are even on some Mexican money.

In March 1947, a few months before the 100th anniversary of the deaths of the *niños*, Harry S. Truman became the first U.S. president to visit Mexico City. The president made an unscheduled stop at Chapultepec. Truman placed a wreath at the monument and stood in silent reverence. Asked by U.S. reporters why he had gone to the monument, Truman said, "Brave men don't belong to any one country. I respect bravery wherever I see it."[31]

THE END OF WAR

By September 14, 1847, U.S. troops occupied Mexico City. It seemed to be a matter of time before a peace treaty would officially end the war. But Mexico's government was in turmoil. No one was sure who was in charge—or who should take responsibility for making peace with the Americans.

President Polk sent Nicholas Trist to negotiate the peace. Trist had been the U.S. consul (or ambassador) to Cuba. He spoke fluent Spanish. But his job was not easy. Almost immediately, Trist argued with General Scott. The general dismissed Trist as the "chief clerk." Eventually, the two put aside their differences and became close friends. But Polk did not like Trist. Their relationship worsened when Polk learned the diplomat had befriended Scott, a Whig rival.[32]

Trist had another problem. He waited for months before he could find a Mexican official willing to talk about a treaty. Once Santa Anna fled the country, a new Mexican government was formed. The new president, former foreign minister Manuel Peña y Peña, was willing to consider the terms of the United States.

But just as Trist was finally making headway, he received an angry letter from Polk. The president had grown tired of waiting for a treaty. He demanded that Trist return to Washington, D.C. He said that if Trist could not get the job done, Polk would send someone else. Trist was not sure what to do. Finally, he chose to ignore the president. Trist met with Mexican officials to finish the peace and secure the land that Polk had long coveted.

THE TREATY OF GUADALUPE HIDALGO

In the end, Mexico had no choice but to accept all of the United States' demands. On February 2, 1848, Trist and his Mexican counterparts signed the Treaty of Guadalupe Hidalgo. It gave the United States undisputed control of Texas at the Rio Grande border. The United States claimed what are now California, New Mexico, Nevada, Utah, most of Arizona and Colorado, and parts of Oklahoma, Kansas, and Wyoming. Most of the tens of thousands of Mexicans who lived in this territory simply stayed on their land.

Altogether, the United States took half of Mexico's territory. The Treaty of Guadalupe Hidalgo was a sweeping success. Still, when Trist returned to Washington, an angry President Polk refused to pay him for his work.

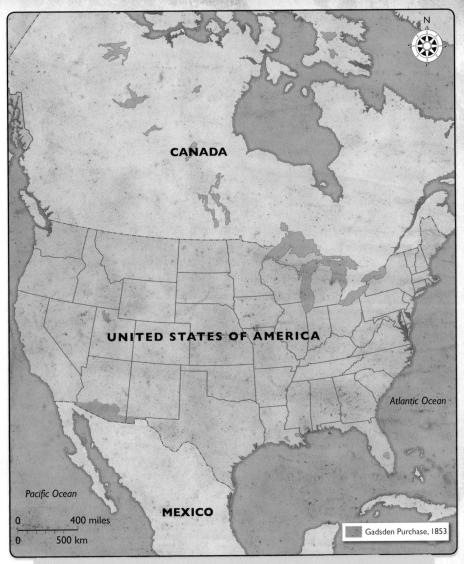

CANADA

UNITED STATES OF AMERICA

Atlantic Ocean

Pacific Ocean

MEXICO

0   400 miles

0   500 km

Gadsden Purchase, 1853

△ The Mexican War forever changed the map of the Americas. The U.S. added 500,000 square miles, including California, New Mexico, Nevada, Utah, most of Arizona and Colorado, and parts of Oklahoma, Kansas, and Wyoming.

The war was over. The United States had added over 500,000 square miles (1.3 million square kilometers) of territory. Next to the Louisiana Purchase, it is the largest addition in the country's history. In return, Mexico received about $18 million—less than half the amount Polk had attempted to pay for the land before the war.

WHAT HAVE WE LEARNED?

At the start of the war, the United States and Mexico were nations headed in different directions. The young United States was expanding. It was giddy with the promise of industrialization and inventions. It had a firm belief in Manifest Destiny, the country's God-given right to occupy more land.

Mexico had won its independence from Spain. But it was still a nation with an unstable government and little economic or technical advancement.

By the war's end, the two countries would be even further apart.

A NATION EXPANDS...

In the United States, the war's outcome was widely cheered. The United States had won its first war fought almost entirely on foreign territory. The U.S. Army swelled from just over 6,000 to more than 115,000 soldiers.

Pioneers quickly settled the new western lands. By the start of the Civil War, more than 4.3 million Americans had moved west of the Mississippi River. In 1849 gold was discovered in California and Nevada, leading to even more westward expansion and a boost to the U.S. economy. Fueled by the locomotive, and buoyed by a resounding war victory, the United States seemed to be a nation on the rise.[1]

...BUT DIVISIONS ARE REVEALED

But the war also revealed deep divisions in the country. The U.S. peace movement continued to vigorously denounce Polk's actions. Led by Congressman Abraham Lincoln, the House of Representatives passed a bill condemning "a war unnecessarily and unconstitutionally begun by the President of the United States."[2]

The war had cost an enormous $75 million—not to mention the nearly 6,000 lives lost in battle and the 11,000 soldiers who died from diseases. Some soldiers wondered if it had been worth the cost. Before becoming an accomplished Civil War general, Ulysses S. Grant was a young lieutenant in the Mexican-American War. Despite the victory, he condemned the war as "one of the most unjust ever waged by a stronger against a weaker nation."[3]

As abolitionists had predicted, the war inflamed the slavery issue. Congress continued to battle over whether the new territories would be slave or free states. Slavery was spreading. Five years after Texas was annexed, one in four Texans was a slave. The new territories were a battleground over slavery—finally erupting with the Civil War.

DEFEAT FOR MEXICO

In some ways, Mexico never recovered from its defeat. The war produced tens of thousands of orphans, widows, and cripples. The heavy U.S. shelling destroyed cities, ports, and roads. The nation's government and economy were in shambles.

But the worst effect on Mexicans was psychological. The once-proud nation was humiliated. It had lost more than 50,000 men and half of its territory. The war became a symbol of weakness among Mexicans.[4]

TIMELINE

1821	Mexico wins its independence from Spain after a 20-year struggle. Mexico takes control of all former Spanish territories, including Texas, California, and most of what is now the western United States.
1836	Mexico's new constitution outlaws slavery in all of its territories. U.S. settlers in Texas declare their independence.
1836 February 23	General Antonio López de Santa Anna leads the Mexican army against a Texas rebellion at the Alamo.
March 6	After a brutal 13-day siege, Santa Anna's 3,000 soldiers win a hard-fought battle, killing 200 Texans.
April 21	Texans, led by General Sam Houston, defeat Santa Anna at the Battle of San Jacinto.
1836	Santa Anna is forced to sign a treaty granting Texas its independence. The Mexican government does not recognize the treaty.
1844	In November, James K. Polk is elected the 11th president of the United States. He promises to annex Texas.
1845 July	Newspaper publisher John O'Sullivan first uses the term "Manifest Destiny" to describe the U.S. belief that it has a God-given right to expand its territory.
October	Polk stations 3,000 troops along the Rio Grande.
November	Polk sends John Slidell to Mexico with orders to buy New Mexico and Texas. The fractured Mexican government refuses to meet with Slidell.
December 29	Texas is annexed as the 28th U.S. state.
1846 January 1	Polk orders General Zachary Taylor to march to the Rio Grande and protect Texas from any invasion by Mexico.
April 25	The Thornton Affair occurs, in which a 2,000-strong Mexican cavalry crosses the Rio Grande and surprises a 70-man U.S. patrol. Captain Seth Thornton and 16 of his men are killed.
May 8	At the Battle of Palo Alto, 2,400 Americans defeat twice as many Mexicans to mark the beginning of the Mexican-American War.
May 11	Declaring that Mexico "shed American blood upon American soil," Polk asks Congress for a declaration of war against Mexico.
May 13	After debating just a few hours, Congress declares war against Mexico.

June 14	In California, U.S. settlers led by Captain John C. Frémont proclaim their independence from Mexico and raise the "Bear Flag." The new Republic of California is later annexed by the United States in August.
July 25	Poet Henry David Thoreau is sent to jail for one night when he refuses to pay his taxes, as an antiwar protest.
August 8	The Wilmot Proviso, which would have outlawed slavery in territories gained during the war, is defeated in the U.S. Congress.
August 15	The United States annexes New Mexico, formerly a Mexican territory.
August 18	After winning the Battle of Santa Fe, General Stephen Kearny occupies the city.
1847 February 22	In the Battle of Buena Vista, General Taylor's army of 4,800 men defeats General Santa Anna's 15,000-man force.
March 9–29	After a landmark naval landing, General Winfield Scott's forces attack Veracruz.
September 10	Sixteen former U.S. soldiers from the Saint Patrick's Battalion—known as San Patricios—are executed as traitors for deserting and joining the Mexican side.
September 12	General Scott and his army occupy Chapultepec. During the battle, six young soldiers, ages 13 to 19, are killed while bravely defending the Mexican flag. They are known as *Los Niños Héroes* and are still celebrated today.
September 14	U.S. troops, led by General Scott, occupy Mexico City.
September 16	Santa Anna resigns as Mexican president.
December 22	Illinois congressman Abraham Lincoln makes a speech opposing the Mexican-American War. He demands that Polk "Show me the spot!" where Thornton's party was ambushed.
1848 February 2	The Mexican-American War ends with the Treaty of Guadalupe Hidalgo. Mexico loses 500,000 square miles (1.3 million square kilometers) of its territory. The United States claims what is now California, New Mexico, Nevada, Utah, most of Arizona and Colorado, and parts of Oklahoma, Kansas, and Wyoming.
November	Zachary Taylor is elected the 12th president of the United States. He dies in office after just one year.
1849	On June 15, former President Polk dies of cholera, just two months after leaving office.

GLOSSARY

abolitionist activist who opposed slavery, especially leading up to the Civil War

adobe clay that forms bricks for houses

ambassador high-ranking diplomatic official

ambush surprise attack

amphibious able to operate both on land and in water

amputation cutting off something, such as a limb

annex take something; to add a territory as part of a country

antibiotic substance or compound that kills or stops the growth of bacteria

aristocrat member of a wealthy, ruling class

artillery large-caliber weapons, like cannons or missile launchers

Aztecs Indian tribe that ruled a vast empire in central Mexico throughout the 14th, 15th, and 16th centuries. The Spanish explorer Hernán Cortés largely wiped out the Aztecs in 1519.

bayonet knife or sword-shaped weapon designed to fit on the muzzle of a gun

blockade act of isolating, closing off, or surrounding a place such as a port or harbor

cavalry soldiers on horseback

chaparral dense forest or vegetation consisting of thick trees or bushes

cholera potentially fatal intestinal infection caused by contaminated water or food. It causes watery diarrhea, vomiting, muscle cramps, and severe dehydration.

civilian anyone who is not a member of the armed forces

coup sudden change of government, usually illegally or by force, often led by a country's military

desert abandon; suddenly leave someone behind

dysentery infection of the intestines causing severe diarrhea

empire large area of land ruled over by a single authority, like an emperor or empress

enlist join the military

fortified strengthened and secured

gallows frame, usually wooden, used for execution by hanging

guerrilla member of an irregular army that often fights stronger, bigger forces and uses tactics like ambushes and surprise attacks

immigrant person who leaves one country to settle permanently in another

impenetrable impossible to break through or enter

incite provoke or urge on

Industrial Revolution period from the late 1700s to the early 1800s when much of the world, led by Great Britain, transformed from agricultural-based economies to factory- and machine-based economies

industrialization process through which a country develops industries, such as factories

malaria disease spread by mosquitoes that causes fever, chills, and other flu-like symptoms. It is still responsible for over one million deaths a year.

Manifest Destiny belief by Americans in the 19th century that they had a God-given right to expand their way of life and their territory across the North American continent from the Atlantic to the Pacific oceans

mestizo slang word used to describe people with a mix of Spanish and Indian ancestry

militia civilians who are trained as soldiers but are not part of the regular army (often volunteers)

missionary someone who works among nonbelievers to spread the message of his or her own religion

mortar high-angle gun with a short barrel that fires shells. Mortars travel over high elevations for a short range.

mountain fever bacterial infection spread by wood ticks

musket long-barreled gun, used primarily from the 16th to 18th centuries

occupation control of a country by military forces of a foreign power

republic state in which power belongs to citizens rather than a king or government; a democracy

roughneck group of rough or violent people

smallpox highly contagious, deadly disease characterized by skin eruptions with pustules and scabs. Once common, smallpox was wiped out in the 1970s.

soldados Spanish term for "soldiers"

sovereign having power over yourself or your country; not controlled by outside forces

tariff tax on imported or exported goods

telegraph messages sent over cables or wires

terrain piece of ground; also, militarily important land

treaty written agreement between two states or countries

typhoid serious intestinal infection caused by bacteria in food or water

Whig Party nineteenth-century U.S. political party formed to oppose the Democratic Party. Whigs were generally against slavery and supported industrialization.

yellow fever deadly infectious disease, usually spread by mosquitoes

NOTES ON SOURCES

A War of Contradictions (pages 4–5)

1. Robert W. Johannsen, "America's Forgotten War," *The Wilson Quarterly* 20 (Spring 1996).
2. David M. Pletcher, "Manifest Destiny: An Ideal or a Justification?" *The U.S.-Mexican War*, http://www.pbs.org/kera/usmexicanwar/. Accessed on March 11, 2011.
3. Johannsen, "America's Forgotten War."
4. Thomas Christensen and Carol Christensen, *The U.S.-Mexican War* (San Francisco: Bay Books, 1998).
5. David J. Weber, "Many Truths Constitute the Past: The Legacy of *the U.S.-Mexican War*," *The U.S.-Mexican War*, http://www.pbs.org/kera/usmexicanwar/. Accessed on March 11, 2011.
6. Robert Ryal Miller, "The War Between the United States and Mexico," *The U.S.-Mexican War*, http://www.pbs.org/kera/usmexicanwar/. Accessed on March 11, 2011.

Tensions Rise (pages 6–13)

1. PBS, "Two Nations' Identities: Looking Forward and Looking Back," *The U.S.-Mexican War*, http://www.pbs.org/kera/usmexicanwar/resources/video_library.html.
2. Timothy Foote, "The Way We Were—and the Way We Went—in 1846: What with the Mexican War, and a Million Square Miles of New Real Estate, Our Westward Destiny Became Highly Manifest," *Smithsonian* (April 1996).
3. Donald Fithian Stevens, *Origins of Instability in Early Republican Mexico* (Durham, NC: Duke University Press, 1991).
4. PBS, "Two Nations' Identities: Looking Forward and Looking Back."
5. Foote, "The Way We Were—and the Way We Went—in 1846."
6. *Ibid.*
7. J. R. Edmondson, *The Alamo Story—From History to Current Conflicts* (Plano, TX: Republic of Texas Press, 2000).
8. Liz Sonneborn, *The Mexican-American War: A Primary Source History of the Expansion of the Western Lands of the United States* (New York: Rosen Publishing Group, 2005).
9. PBS, "Biographies: Stephen F. Austin," *The U.S.-Mexican War*, http://www.pbs.org/kera/usmexicanwar/biographies/stephen_austin.html.
10. *Ibid.*
11. Martha Manchaca, *Recovering History, Constructing Race: The Indian, Black, and White Roots of Mexican Americans* (Austin, TX: University of Texas Press, 2001).
12. *Ibid.*
13. Frances Calderon de la Barca, *Life in Mexico* (1843; repr., Los Angeles: University of California Press, 1982).
14. *Ibid.*
15. *Ibid.*
16. PBS, "Mexico in the Shadow of Its Own History," *The U.S.-Mexican War*, http://www.pbs.org/kera/usmexicanwar/resources/video_library.html. Accessed on March 11, 2011.
17. Calderon, *Life in Mexico*.
18. PBS, "Mexico in the Shadow of Its Own History."
19. Morris Schaff, *Etna and Kirkersville* (Boston: Houghton, Mifflin, 1905).
20. Foote, "The Way We Were—and the Way We Went—in 1846."
21. Schaff, *Etna and Kirkersville*.
22. *Ibid.*
23. Schaff, *Etna and Kirkersville*.

Countdown to War (pages 14–23)

1. Foote, "The Way We Were—and the Way We Went—in 1846."

2. Ray Allen Billington and Martin Ridge, *Westward Expansion: A History of the American Frontier*, 6th ed. (Albuquerque: University of New Mexico Press, 2001).

3. *Ibid.*

4. Pletcher, "Manifest Destiny: An Ideal or a Justification?"

5. PBS, "Mexico After Independence: Much Land, Few Settlers," *The U.S.-Mexican War*, http://www.pbs.org/kera/usmexicanwar/. Accessed on March 11, 2011.

6. Billington and Ridge, *Westward Expansion: A History of the American Frontier*.

7. Foote, "The Way We Were—and the Way We Went—in 1846."

8. "McNeil's Travels in 1849 to, through, and from the Gold Regions in California," in *California As I Saw It: First-Person Narratives of California's Early Years, 1849-1900* (Washington, DC: Library of Congress, General Collections and Rare Book and Special Collections Division, 1997).

9. Steven Mintz, "Manifest Destiny," Digital History, http://www.digitalhistory.uh.edu/historyonline/us17.cfm. Accessed on March 12, 2011.

10. Foote, "The Way We Were—and the Way We Went—in 1846."

11. James M. McCaffrey, "Life in the U.S. Army," *The U.S.-Mexican War*, http://www.pbs.org/kera/usmexicanwar/. Accessed on March 12, 2011.

12. Johannsen, "America's Forgotten War."

13. Howard Zinn, "We Take Nothing By Conquest, Thank God," in *A People's History of the United States* (New York: Harper Perennial, 2003), http://www.historyisaweapon.com/defcon1/zinntak8.html. Accessed on March 12, 2011.

14. Johannsen, "America's Forgotten War."

15. John S. D. Eisenhower and Arnold C. Holeywell, *So Far from God: The U.S. War with Mexico, 1846-1848* (New York: Random House, 1989).

16. Zinn, "We Take Nothing By Conquest, Thank God."

17. Steven Mintz, "War Fever and Antiwar Protests," Digital History, http://www.digitalhistory.uh.edu/database/article_display.cfm?HHID=318. Accessed on March 12, 2011.

18. *Ibid.*

19. *Ibid.*

20. Douglas Card, "We Forget That Lincoln Opposed a War, Too," *Register-Guard*, January 7, 2009.

21. Mintz, "War Fever and Antiwar Protests."

The War in Texas and Mexico (pages 24–39)

1. Son of the South, "Civil War Medicine," http://www.sonofthesouth.net/leefoundation/civil-war-medicine.htm. Accessed on March 12, 2011.

2. D. H. Hill, "The Army in Texas," *Southern Quarterly Review 9* (April 1846).

3. N. C. Brooks, *A Complete History Of The Mexican War* (1849; repr., Scholar's Bookshelf, 2006).

4. Heidler and Heidler, *Daily Lives of Civilians in Wartime Early America*.

5. David Stephen Heidler and Jeanne T. Heidler, eds., *Daily Lives of Civilians in Wartime Early America: From the Colonial Era to the Civil War* (Westport, CT: Greenwood Press, 2007).

6. Suzann Ledbetter, *Shady Ladies: Nineteen Surprising and Rebellious American Women* (New York: Forge Books), 2006.

7. *Ibid.*

8. Heidler and Heidler, *Daily Lives of Civilians in Wartime Early America*.

9. Ledbetter, Shady Ladies.

10. *Ibid.*

11. PBS, "The Capture of Monterrey," *The U.S.-Mexican War*, http://www.pbs.org/kera/usmexicanwar/. Accessed on March 12, 2011.

12. Christopher Dishman, *A Perfect Gibraltar: The Battle for Monterrey, Mexico* (Norman, OK: University of Oklahoma Press, 2010).

13. Paul S. Boyer, Clifford Clark, Sandra Hawley, Joseph F. Kett, and Andrew Rieser, *The Enduring Vision: A History of the American People*, vol. 1, To 1877 (Boston: Houghton Mifflin, 2007).

14. Hill, "The Army in Texas."
15. Ibid.
16. Hill, "The Army in Texas."
17. PBS, "The Battle of Buena Vista," The U.S.-Mexican War, http://www.pbs.org/kera/usmexicanwar/. Accessed on March 12, 2011.
18. Descendants of Mexican War Veterans, "Soldiers and Soldados, The US-Mexican War," http://www.dmwv.org/mexwar/mexwar1.htm. Accessed on March 12, 2011.
19. American Military and Navy History, "Weapons of the Mexican War 1846–1847," http://www.americanmilitaryhistorymsw.com/blog/526859-weapons-of-the-mexican-war-18461847/. Accessed on March 12, 2011.
20. Ibid.
21. Descendants of Mexican War Veterans, "Soldiers and Soldados, The US-Mexican War."
22. PBS, "The Battle of Buena Vista."
23. Ibid.
24. Ibid.
25. Daniel T. Kuehl, "'Double-Shot Your Guns and Give 'Em Hell!' Braxton Bragg and the War in Mexico," Civil War History 37, no. 1 (1991).
26. Leonard V. Huber, "A Cover Forwarded by the 'Delta Express,'" Stamps, May 11, 1996.
27. Johannsen, "America's Forgotten War."
28. Huber, "A Cover Forwarded by the 'Delta Express'."
29. Ibid.
30. Ibid.

Go West! (pages 40–49)
1. Steven Mintz, "Westward Expansion," Digital History, http://www.digitalhistory.uh.edu/database/subtitles.cfm?TitleID=57. Accessed on March 12, 2011.
2. Ibid.
3. Ibid.
4. Matthew Kachur and Jon Sterngass, The Mexican-American War (Milwaukee, WI: World Almanac Library, 2011).
5. California As I Saw It.
6. Steven Mintz, "Life on the Trail," Digital History, http://www.digitalhistory.uh.edu/database/article_

display.cfm?HHID=310. Accessed on March 12, 2011.
7. Ibid.
8. Steven Mintz, "Life on the Trail," Digital History, http://www.digitalhistory.uh.edu/database/article_display.cfm?HHID=310. Accessed on March 12, 2011.
9. Ibid.
10. Foote, "The Way We Were—and the Way We Went—in 1846."
11. Steven Mintz, "The Donner Party," Digital History, http://www.digitalhistory.uh.edu/database/article_display.cfm?HHID=303. Accessed on March 12, 2011.
12. Ibid.
13. George R. Stewart, Ordeal by Hunger: The Story of the Donner Party (1936; repr., New York: Houghton Mifflin, 1988).
14. Mintz, "The Donner Party."
15. Stewart, Ordeal by Hunger.
16. Descendants of Mexican War Veterans, "The Conquest of California, The US-Mexican War," http://www.dmwv.org/mexwar/mexwar1.htm. Accessed on March 13, 2011.
17. Foote, "The Way We Were—and the Way We Went—in 1846."
18. PBS, "Biographies: John C. Frémont," The U.S.-Mexican War, http://www.pbs.org/kera/usmexicanwar/biographies/stephen_austin.html. Accessed on March 13, 2011.

The Fall of Mexico (pages 50–65)
1. Boyer, Clark, Hawley, Kett, and Rieser, The Enduring Vision.
2. Descendants of Mexican War Veterans, "The War in Central Mexico, The US-Mexican War," http://www.dmwv.org/mexwar/mexwar1.htm. Accessed on March 13, 2011.
3. Britannica Concise Encyclopedia, s.v. "Winfield Scott," http://www.britannica.com/EBchecked/topic/529654/Winfield-Scott. Accessed on March 13, 2011.
4. Descendants of Mexican War Veterans, "The War in Central Mexico, The US-Mexican War," http://www.dmwv.org/mexwar/mexwar1.htm. Accessed on March 13, 2011.
5. Ramón Alacaraz and Albert C. Ramsey,

trans., *The Other Side: Or Notes for the History of the War Between Mexico and the United States Written in Mexico* (New York: J. Wiley and Sons, 1850).

6. *Ibid.*
7. *Ibid.*
8. Donald S. Frazier, "Army Life: Mexican Army," *The U.S.-Mexican War*, http://www.pbs.org/kera/usmexicanwar/. Accessed on March 12, 2011.
9. PBS, "The Battle of Cerro Gordo," *The U.S.-Mexican War*, http://www.pbs.org/kera/usmexicanwar/. Accessed on March 13, 2011.
10. Sonneborn, *The Mexican-American War*.
11. Eisenhower and Holeywell, *So Far from God*.
12. Randy L. Sible, "The Life of Antonio Lopez de Santa Anna: Savior, Emperor, President, and Dictator," Latin American Studies, http://www.latinamericanstudies.org/mex-war/santa-anna2.htm. Accessed on March 13, 2011.
13. James Callaghan, "The San Patricios (The American-Mexican War and a Renegade Called John O'Reilly)," *American Heritage* (November 1995).
14. Foote, "The Way We Were—and the Way We Went—in 1846."
15. Callaghan, "The San Patricios."
16. *Ibid.*
17. *Ibid.*
18. David A. Clary, Eagles and Empire: *The United States, Mexico, and the Struggle for a Continent* (New York: Bantam Books, 2009).
19. Dennis J. Wunn, *San Patricio Soldiers: Mexico's Foreign Legion* (El Paso, TX: Texas Western Press, 1985).
20. Eisenhower and Holeywell, *So Far from God*.
21. John George Nicolay and John Hay, eds., *Abraham Lincoln: Complete Works, Comprising His Speeches, Letters, State Papers, and Miscellaneous Writings*, vol. 1 (Charleston, SC: Nabu Press, 2010).
22. Samuel Chamberlain, "My Confession: Recollections of a Rogue," *Life*, July 23, 1956.
23. Descendants of Mexican War Veterans, "The War in Central Mexico."
24. David W. Tschanz, "Yellow Fever and the Strategy of *the Mexican-American War*," Montana State University, http://entomology.montana.edu/historybug/mexwar/mexwar.htm.
25. Tschanz, "Yellow Fever and the Strategy of *the Mexican-American War*."
26. *Ibid.*
27. Descendants of Mexican War Veterans, "The War in Central Mexico."
28. PBS, "The Battle of Chapultepec and 'Los Niños Héroes,'" *The U.S.-Mexican War*, http://www.pbs.org/kera/usmexicanwar/resources/video_library.html. Accessed on March 11, 2011.
29. Jim Tuck, "Mexico's Niños Heroes ("Heroic Children"): Reality or Myth?" Mexconnect, http://www.mexconnect.com/articles/313-mexico-s-niños-heroes-heroic-children-reality-or-myth. Accessed on March 13, 2011.
30. Mexonline, "Los Niños Héroes," http://www.mexonline.com/history-ninosheroes.htm. Accessed on March 13, 2011.
31. Tuck, "Mexico's Niños Heroes."
32. Frederic D. Schwarz, "Great Scott (Gen. Winfield Scott's Actions During the End of *the Mexican-American War* in 1847)," *American Heritage* (April 1997).

What Have We Learned? (pages 66–67)
1. PBS, "Two Nations' Identities."
2. *Journal of the House of Representatives of the United States*, 1847–1848, Monday, January 3, 1848, http://memory.loc.gov/cgi-bin/query/r?ammem/hlaw:@field(DOCID+@lit(hj04321)), Accessed on March 13, 2011.
3. Ulysses S. Grant, Personal Memoirs. (New York: C. L. Webster and Company, 1885–86), http://www.bartleby.com/1011/. Accessed on March 11, 2011.
4. Weber, "Many Truths Constitute the Past."

BIBLIOGRAPHY

BOOKS

Alcaraz, Ramón, and Albert C. Ramsey, trans. *The Other Side: Or Notes for the History of the War Between Mexico and the United States.* New York: J. Wiley and Sons, 1850.

Boyer, Paul S., Clifford Clark, Joseph F. Kett, and Neal Salisbury. *The Enduring Vision: A History of the American People.* Vol. 1, To 1877. Boston: Houghton Mifflin, 2007.

California As I Saw It: First-Person Narratives of California's Early Years, 1849–1900. Washington, D.C.: Library of Congress, General Collections and Rare Book and Special Collections Division, 1997.

Eisenhower, John S. D. *So Far from God: The U.S. War with Mexico, 1846–1848.* New York: Random House, 1989.

Greenwood, Barbara. *A Pioneer Sampler: The Daily Life of a Pioneer Family in 1840.* Boston: Houghton Mifflin, 1998.

Heidler, David Stephen, and Jeanne T. Heidler, eds. *Daily Lives of Civilians in Wartime Early America: From the Colonial Era to the Civil War.* Westport, CT: Greenwood Press, 2007.

Joseph, Gilbert Michael, and Timothy J. Henderson, eds. *The Mexico Reader: History, Culture, Politics.* Durham, NC: Duke University Press, 2002.

Schaff, Morris. *Etna and Kirkersville.* Boston: Houghton Mifflin, 1905.

Sonneborn, Liz. *The Mexican-American War: A Primary Source History of the Expansion of the Western Lands of the United States.* New York: Rosen Publishing Group, 2005.

ARTICLES

Callaghan, James. "The San Patricios (The American-Mexican War and a Renegade Called John O'Reilly)." *American Heritage* (November 1995).

Card, Douglas. "We Forget That Lincoln Opposed a War, Too." *Register-Guard*, January 7, 2009.

Chamberlain, Sam. "My Confession: Recollections of a Rogue." *Life*, July 23, 1956.

Foote, Timothy. "The Way We Were—and the Way We Went—in 1846: What with the Mexican War, and a Million Square Miles of New Real Estate, Our Westward Destiny Became Highly Manifest." *Smithsonian*, April 1996, xx [page #s].

Hill, D. H. "The Army in Texas." *Southern Quarterly Review 9* (April 1846): xx [page #s].

Johannsen, Robert W. "America's Forgotten War." *The Wilson Quarterly 20* (Spring 1996): xx [page #s].

Tschanz, David W. "Yellow Fever and the Strategy of the Mexican-American War." Montana State University, http://entomology.montana.edu/historybug/mexwar/mexwar.htm.

WEBSITES

Descendants of Mexican War Veterans
www.dmwv.org/mexwar/mexwar1.htm

Digital History
www.digitalhistory.uh.edu

PBS: The U.S.-Mexican War
www.pbs.org/kera/usmexicanwar/

FIND OUT MORE

BOOKS

Shaara, Jeff. *Gone for Soldiers: A Novel of the Mexican War.* New York: Ballantine, 2000.

In this historical novel, Pulitzer Prize–winning author Shaara mixes real war figures like Winfield Scott with fictional characters as he intertwines the history of the Mexican-American War with the careers of officers who continued into the Civil War.

WEBSITES

www.thealamo.org

Check out the official site of the Alamo, which is a major San Antonio tourist attraction.

www.dmwv.org/mexwar/mexwar1.htm

This Descendents of Mexican War Veterans site offers more than just a history of the war. Read journals and letters from soldiers who fought in the war. Learn about the Veteran Graves Registry Project.

DVDS

American Experience: The Donner Party (Alexandria, Va.: PBS; distributed by Warner Home Video, 1992).

This PBS-produced movie re-creates the Donner party's doomed journey, using family journals, newspaper accounts, and interviews with historians and descendants.

You can view the film at www.pbs.org/wgbh/americanexperience/films/donner/player/.

History Channel Presents: The Mexican-American War (New York: History/A&E Television Networks; distributed by New Video, 2008).

This feature-length special reexamines the controversial war. It features lavish reenactments and interviews with both Mexican and U.S. historians.

INDEX